THE AIRBRUSH
IN ARCHITECTURAL
ILLUSTRATION

THE AIRBRUSH IN ARCHITECTURAL ILLUSTRATION

Tibor K. Karsai

 VAN NOSTRAND REINHOLD
New York

Printed in Hong Kong

Designed by Rose Delia Vasquez

Van Nostrand Reinhold
115 Fifth Avenue
New York, New York 10003

Van Nostrand Reinhold (International) Limited
11 New Fetter Lane
London EC4P 4EE, England

Van Nostrand Reinhold
480 La Trobe Street
Melbourne, Victoria 3000, Australia

Macmillan of Canada
Division of Canada Publishing Corporation
164 Commander Boulevard
Agincourt, Ontario M1S 3C7, Canada

16 15 14 13 12 11 10 9 8 7 6 5 4 3 2 1

Library of Congress Cataloging-in-Publication Data

Karsai, Tibor K., 1937–
    The airbrush in architectural illustration.

    Bibliography: p.
    Includes index.
    1. Architectural drawing—Technique.   2. Airbrush
art.   I. Title.
NA2726.K37   1989   720'.28'4   88-5527
ISBN 0-442-24690-0

To my wife, Gizi, and our daughter, Liza, for putting up with me, the most difficult task of all.

CONTENTS

Preface   **ix**

Acknowledgments   **xi**

1. **AIRBRUSHES AND OTHER EQUIPMENT**   **1**
   The Airbrush   3
   The Air Supply   9
   Media and Grounds   11
   Other Tools and Supplies   15

2. **LEARNING THE TECHNIQUE: BASIC EXERCISES**   **23**
   Tips for Operating the Airbrush   25
   Warm-Up Exercises: Dots, Lines, Tone   26
   Exercises in Solid Geometric Forms:
     Cube, Cylinder, Sphere   30

3. **ARCHITECTURAL APPLICATIONS: ADVANCED EXERCISES**   **43**
   Basic Surface Treatments: Precast Concrete and Stucco, Brick, Marble   45
   Three-Dimensional Surface Treatments:
     Building Detail, Alternative Method, Three-Dimensionality in Brick, Marble   51
   Rendering Important Details: A Corner Window, A Glass Facade, An Afternoon Sky   60

4. **DEMONSTRATIONS FROM THE PROJECT FILE**   **77**
   School Addition   78
   Medical Building   82
   Airport Hotel   89
   Glass and Concrete Office Building   95
   Brick Office Building   100
   A Downtown Plaza   107

5. **A PORTFOLIO OF ARCHITECTURAL ILLUSTRATION**   **115**

Bibliography   **161**

Index   **163**

PREFACE

Since its development in the nineteenth century, the airbrush has played an increasingly large role in both the fine arts and commercial fields. Its versatility has enabled artists to achieve a wide variety of hues and textures quickly and efficiently. Painstaking and time-consuming rendering becomes fast and pleasurable to produce when using an airbrush.

You see the results of airbrushing all around you, probably without realizing it. Illustrations created for advertising, packaging that is photoretouched, and special film effects—all rely on the basic airbrush technique somewhere in their processes. Used alone or in combination with other methods, the airbrush has become an important tool in my field, architectural illustration.

In architecture, the portrait of a building is often the first look at a new project presented to the general public or the various government agencies. The building must be realistically represented if the project is to succeed—presenting the architect's ideas accurately to the client, securing funding and licenses from government agencies, attracting buyers and tenants, and so on. For creating these illustrations, the airbrush is indispensable. With it, the artist can speedily and accurately render such complicated surfaces as bricks, glass, marble, materials containing aggregate, granite, or travertine. Without it, such surface depictions would take hours of work with the stipple brush. These surface effects are not confined to the world of the architectural illustrator. They make up part of the visual vocabulary of airbrush artists in many other fields as well.

Many artists are intimidated by the airbrush, but working with one need not be a frightening experience. With diligence, a little patience, and practice most artists can soon become reasonably well-versed in its many applications. This book is intended for those artists who have already overcome their resistance, if they had any, to the airbrush technique. It is not a basic how-to book for beginners on the technique of airbrushing. There are many such books available, some of which are listed in the bibliography.

While in chapters 1 and 2, I do include some basic information on equipment and technique, for the most part this is intended merely as a refresher, with the primary focus on how the technique is used to achieve the textures and effects of architectural work. In translating this technique to paper, I have drawn on more than twenty-five years of professional experience in this field. In the pages that follow, I will share my own experience with you, but your experience and enthusiasm, your willingness to experiment, will also determine how successful this book is as a teaching tool.

ACKNOWLEDGMENTS

Creating this book was a challenge and a great learning experience. Along the way, I was afforded the privilege of meeting and working with some gifted people.

I would like to extend my thanks and appreciation to Martina D'Alton for her assistance and expertise in organizing the art and the manuscript. I would also like to express my gratitude to the following: the people at Van Nostrand Reinhold, particularly Wendy Lochner, Marie Finamore, and Ed Grazda, for their endless patience and encouragement; the architects, designers, and clients whose continued support enabled me to produce this book; and to Neil Green and David Lazansky, for their technical support and for keeping me informed of developments in hardware, paint, and equipment. Last, I wish to thank my daughter, Liza Karsai, for her invaluable editorial contribution to this book.

AIRBRUSHES AND OTHER EQUIPMENT

Like any artist's studio, the airbrush studio requires stocking with certain basic equipment. This chapter will give you a checklist overview of these supplies, beginning with the airbrush itself.

THE AIRBRUSH

The airbrush is really nothing more than an atomizer. Attached to a source of compressed air, it creates a fine spray of paint that can be applied evenly to any surface.

There are different kinds of airbrushes, and, as with any tool used by an artist, choice is dictated by both personal preference and the nature of the work at hand. The ergonomics of the airbrush—the way it fits the hand and is balanced—will guide personal preference.

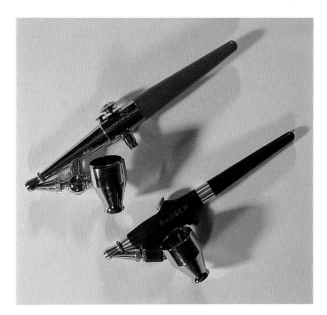

Fig. 1-1. The varying ergonomics of airbrushes: the Paasche H and the Badger 350 airbrushes. Nearly identical in design, the H is larger and perceptibly heavier than the Badger. Notice the different angles of the finger levers. The angle at which the cups attach is also slightly different. The H cup is less likely to spill when poised over horizontal surfaces, whereas the Badger is better for vertical or nearly vertical surfaces. The color cups are interchangeable, adding to the versatility of the airbrushes.

Airbrushes designed to accomplish the same task can feel completely different. One may be heavier or differently balanced than the other. Many manufacturers also offer separate models for right- and left-handed people. If the majority of your work is large scale, there are appropriately sized airbrushes, with large-capacity reservoirs for the medium you use. For intricate, detailed freehand work, there are airbrushes specifically designed for that purpose.

The two basic types of airbrush are single action and double action. They are distinguished by their triggering mechanisms. In a single-action airbrush, the index finger depresses the lever to control the flow of air. In a double-action model, the finger lever is pressed down to control air flow and pulled back to control color flow (the volume of paint), allowing for an infinite number of combinations and spray patterns. Single-action airbrushes also vary according to whether the air and medium are externally mixed (atomized just outside the tip), or internally mixed (atomized inside the airbrush tip).

Single-action, external-mix airbrushes are known as single-action diffusers and are actually like miniature spray guns. Color flow is controlled by turning the nozzle clockwise to increase volume, counterclockwise to decrease volume. These are relatively large airbrushes suitable for large-scale work. They are simply made and easily operated and cleaned. Most have interchangeable spray-tip assemblies of fine, medium, and coarse designations. Because they produce a more discernible dot pattern, they cannot compete with the more sophisticated double-action airbrushes used for extremely delicate freehand work, but I prefer them for most applications in architectural illustration, especially when working with acrylic paints. In fact, most of the illustrations and exercises in this book were done with a single-action diffuser, in this case, the Paasche Model H airbrush, fitted with #1, #3, and #5 spray-tip assemblies for fine, medium, and coarse work. I consider this airbrush the workhorse of my studio. Not only can this airbrush be used for a wide range of effects, but it is easy to clean, with an easily removable needle assembly. Replacement parts are also readily available.

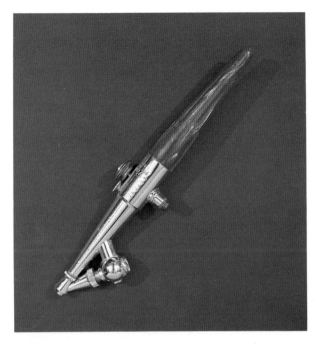

Fig. 1-4. The Paasche Model H single-action diffuser.

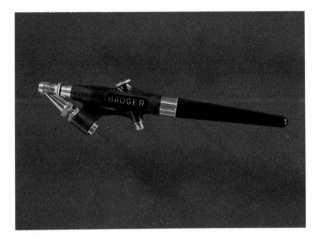

Fig. 1-2. The Badger 350 single-action airbrush.

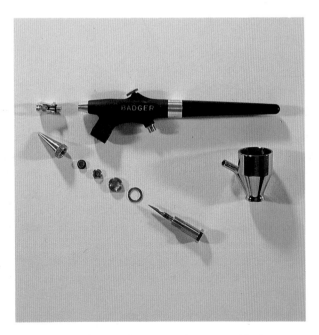

Fig. 1-3. The Badger 350 disassembled.

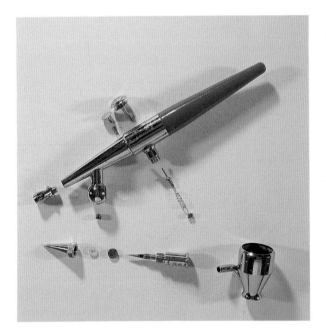

Fig. 1-5. The Paasche Model H disassembled. All single-action diffusers are constructed in a similar manner.

With single-action internal mix airbrushes, the index finger controls the air flow just as it does in the single-action diffuser. Color flow is controlled somewhat differently, however. A nut or "wheel" at the rear of the airbrush is turned to move the needle forward or backward in relation to the nozzle. This opens or closes the passage, allowing more or less color to flow. The air supply is diffused by holes in the air cap, thus reducing direct air pressure on artwork. The reduced air pressure decreases the risk of a ripple effect—blowing accumulated paint uncontrollably over the work surface. One disadvantage, however, is that acrylics are more difficult and time-consuming to clean from single-action internal-mix airbrushes.

Double-action airbrushes are the most versatile. They are also more complex, more expensive, and more difficult to operate than either of the single-action airbrushes. With a double-action airbrush, the index finger controls both air and color flow from a single finger lever—pressed down to release air, then pulled back to release medium, permitting infi-

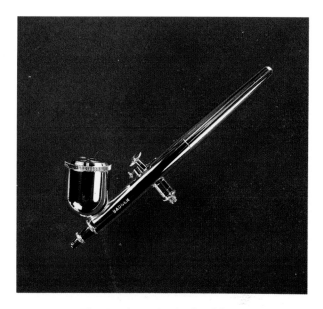

Fig. 1-7. The Badger GFX double-action airbrush with gravity feed.

nite control. On some airbrushes, the backward travel of the needle can be limited by a knurled wheel at the rear tip. This helps maintain a preset color flow, to achieve uniform coverage. The artist has complete freedom to vary the spray in a single stroke, from a tone to a coarse stipple. One feature found on all double-action and most single-action, needle-in-body airbrushes is the adjustable threaded air cap. Screwing it in or out modifies the aperture around the spray tip, giving precise control of stipple effects at low air pressures. This function varies depending on the manufacturer and recent advances in airbrush design.

For very fine, detailed, small-scale work, there is a turbine-driven double-action airbrush that is used by many professionals: the Paasche Model AB. This airbrush is unique. No other manufacturer has yet produced a model based on the same design. On it, the finger level controls a split supply of air that both drives the turbine and blasts past the

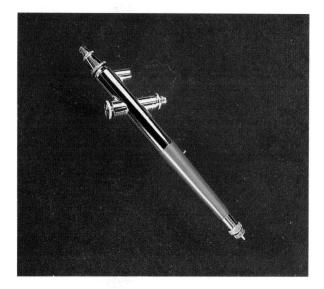

Fig. 1-6. The Badger Model 200 single-action internal-mix airbrush.

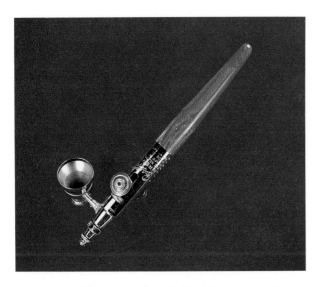

Fig. 1-8. *The Paasche V double-action airbrush. When the original color-cup holder wore out, I had it modified by brazing a Thayer & Chandler Model A tubular fitting to the body of the Paasche. Although it now accepts only Thayer & Chandler color cups, it still works well for fine detail work.*

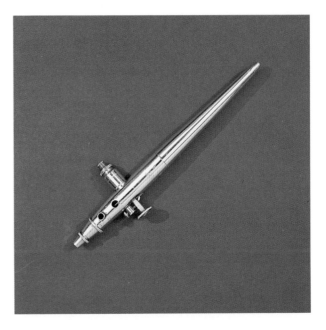

Fig. 1-10. *The Thayer & Chandler Model A double-action airbrush, suitable for extremely fine detail work.*

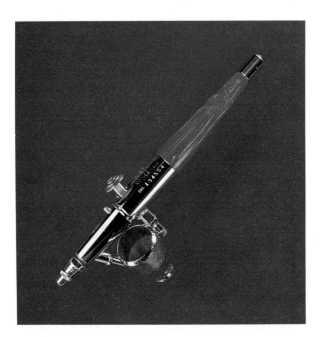

Fig. 1-9. *The Paasche VL, a large double-action airbrush.*

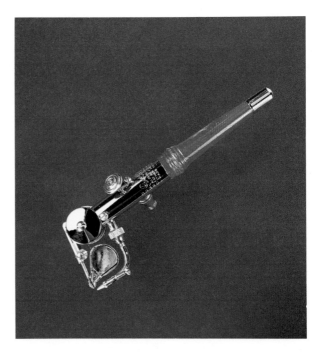

Fig. 1-11. *Paasche Model AB turbine-driven double-action airbrush.*

needle. The turbine moves the needle back and forth at a high rate of speed. At each stroke, the needle passes through the color cup, where it picks up a minute quantity of medium, and then carries it into the air stream, which blows the medium onto the artwork. Such a minute quantity of color is picked up at each stroke that very delicate gradations of tone are possible. The air supply is regulated by a set screw, known as a stipple adjustment, at the rear of the nozzle.

Because of its complexity, the Paasche AB is the most difficult airbrush to learn to use. Yet, mastering and maintaining the Paasche AB is well worth it if delicate work is your stock in trade. Some of the difficulty can be reduced through meticulous maintenance. The Paasche AB needs frequent cleaning, for example. Even the smallest bit of dried paint on the needle and bearing assembly can throw it off, resulting in uncontrolled sputter and irregular color flow. The needle, which runs at ten to fifteen thousand strokes per minute, must be kept well lubricated. The medium acts as a lubricant, so the color cup should never be allowed to empty completely. Operating this airbrush dry even for a very short time can cause as much damage as a car running without oil. The turbine, too, must be kept well lubricated. There are two lube cups that should be kept filled with lubricant or else the turbine bearings will wear out, producing uneven rpms and color flow.

Owning and operating this airbrush can be both exhilarating and exasperating to the point of mental collapse. It has been around since the early 1900s however, and will probably survive unchanged into the next century, until space-age technology can come up with something better.

In considering the many airbrushes available, you should look at and handle several makes of each kind before settling on the right one for you. Once you have decided on the appropriate and most compatible brush for

you, be certain to buy a stock of user-replaceable parts, such as needles, nozzles, air valves, and air-valve springs. These items are easily damaged with use, and of course they do wear out in time. Few things are more frustrating than needing a part at a crucial moment in a project. Keep a stock of spare parts on hand, and you will not have to face this problem.

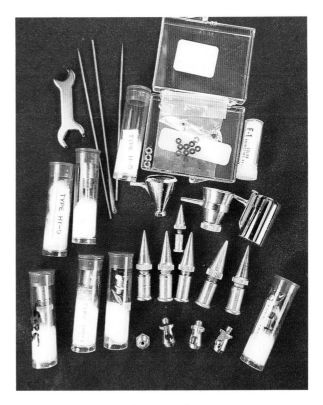

Fig. 1-12. Bits and pieces from my spare-parts repair kit: needles for double-action airbrushes, gaskets and air-valve parts, color cups, and spray-tip assemblies for single- and double-action airbrushes of various sizes.

A Sampling of Airbrushes

Today there is a wide range of airbrushes from many different manufacturers—Badger, Chandler, DeVilbiss, Iwata, Paasche, Thayer & Chandler, and Wold, to name a few of the better-known ones. Spare parts and replacements, once a primary consideration in choosing an airbrush, are much more readily available than they once were, from many suppliers. The following list is just a sampling of the airbrushes that have worked consistently well in my experience as an architectural illustrator.

Single-action airbrushes
    External mix (diffusers)
        Badger 350
        Binks Wren
        Paasche (H and F series models)
    Internal Mix
        Badger 200
        Wold (K and J series models)

Double-action airbrushes
    Badger GFX with gravity feed
    Efbe (C1 and C2 series; B1 and B2 series)
    Grafo (I, II, IIB, IIC, III models)
    Paasche (V1, V2, VL, V-Junior models)
    Wold (A models)

Specialty airbrushes
    Turbine-driven, double-action: Paasche AB
    Air eraser: Paasche AEC

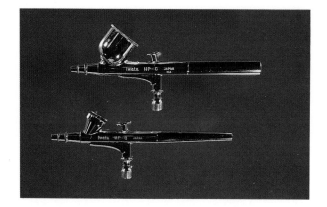

Fig. 1-13. Iwata HP-C and Iwata HP-B. The Iwata HP-C is a double-action airbrush with a permanently attached gravity-feed cup. The Iwata HP-B is a small equivalent of the HP-C. It is a fine double-action airbrush intended for highly detailed work.

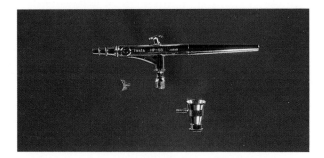

Fig. 1-14. Iwata HP-SB double-action airbrush. Its unusual feature is that its color cup can be attached to either side of the airbrush. The HP-SB is suitable for extremely fine work.

Fig. 1-15. Top view of the Iwata HP-SB, showing color cup attached on the right side and a chrome plug sealing the left attachment port.

Fig. 1-16. *Iwata HP-BC2, a precision-built medium-size double-action airbrush. The knurled knob at the rear of the airbrush is a preset color volume adjustment. This airbrush is suitable for a wide range of applications.*

Fig. 1-17. *The Iwata HP-BC2 with a Paasche Model H color cup attached.*

Fig. 1-18. *The Holbein YT-02, a large single-action, needle-in-body airbrush.*

Fig. 1-19. *The color cups of the Holbein YT-02 attach with a threaded friction wheel, preventing accidental spills. This airbrush is suitable for hobbies, large-scale artwork, and covering large areas.*

THE AIR SUPPLY

Trouble-free operation of the airbrush requires clean, moisture-free, pressurized air. There are several different sources of air supply, from the simplest—cans of propellant—to the most sophisticated—electrically powered air compressors. The choice depends on the work you do, the kind of studio space you have, and the amount of money you are prepared to spend.

Small cans of propellant, although expensive, are fine for the occasional user of an airbrush or for a very small job in the airbrush studio. They are readily available in most art supply stores. They deliver a small amount of pressurized air, lasting anywhere from five minutes to four hours depending on the size and kind of airbrush and the size of the can. Because the air hose cannot be attached directly to the can, you will need a reusable pressure-tank valve. As the can empties, the pressure drops slowly. Pressure also drops if the can gets very cold, which happens as you use it. Stop every now and then and let it warm to room temperature again.

Another portable, nonpowered source of air is the cylinder of compressed gas—carbon dioxide (CO_2) or nitrogen. I have used CO_2 successfully in the past, but some artists prefer to use nitrogen. Either kind, however, is quiet and delivers clean, oil-free and moisture-free air.

If there is a drawback, it is that the cylinders need to be refilled. Making arrangements for pickup and delivery from your supplier will have to become part of your studio routine. It helps to keep a spare filled tank on hand. You will also need to purchase and attach an air-pressure regulator and indicator, which can be expensive.

Another source of pressurized air is the electrically powered air compressor. Today's models provide years of trouble-free operation. The newest ones are fairly quiet and relatively easy to move around. They come in various sizes. Small models will power a single airbrush and supply air pressures of about 30 pounds per square inch (psi), adequate for the average studio work. Larger, more sophisticated models deliver air at higher pressures.

Fig. 1-21. Medium-size compressed gas tank with regulator and pressure indicator attached. A Paasche braided air hose and an Iwata coiled plastic air hose are visible.

With them, you can have several airbrushes running simultaneously and can use large airbrushes to cover large areas. High pressure is also needed to spread thick medium—pea-soup consistency—over existing painted areas. Most of these compressors come equipped with compressed air reservoirs, automatic return valves that turn the compressor on when air pressure in the reservoir falls below a preset level, and pressure regulators equipped with a moisture trap.

If you live in a humid climate and do not have a moisture trap, you should definitely add one. Without it, moisture that condenses in the air hose will interrupt the air flow and the airbrush will sputter intermittently. Uncontrolled irregular water droplets will be blown onto your work surface, not only ruining the work at hand, but also damaging the air-valve system and corroding the air-valve spring. A moisture trap will prevent this from happening.

Fig. 1-20. Badger canned propellant.

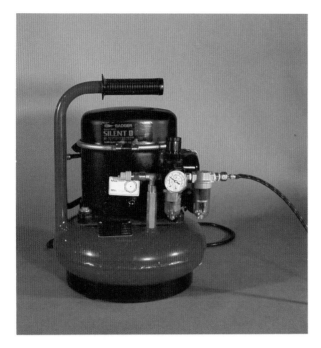

Fig. 1-22. *The Badger Silent-II air compressor: front view.*

Fig. 1-23. *The Badger Silent-II air compressor: back view.*

MEDIA AND GROUNDS

There is a veritable treasure trove of media available for today's airbrush artist. Colors can be produced with inks, dyes, acrylics, oils, and watercolors formulated with organic and synthetic pigments. Some are manufactured specifically for the airbrush; others can be adapted to airbrush use with proper dilution. In fact, almost anything dissolved in liquid can be used in an appropriately sized airbrush. It just has to be diluted and small-particled enough to pass through the airbrush without clogging the works.

Among the traditional media are the water-based paints such as watercolor, gouache, and casein. These are available in tube, cake, or jar form, which must then be diluted with water to the proper consistency for the airbrush you use: very thin, dilute washes for small airbrushes, thicker for large airbrushes. Be aware that the earth-tone colors—ochres and browns, especially—contain coarse pigment particles that are likely to clog the airbrush passages. You should confine their use to the largest, simplest, easiest-to-clean airbrushes. Also, be aware that the best-quality colors, especially among the watercolors, have the finest pigment particles. They also happen to be the most expensive, although a little goes a long way.

Fig. 1-24. *Inks.*

Fig. 1-25. Badger Air-Opaque liquid acrylics.

Fig.1-26. Dr. P.H. Martins synchromatic watercolors.

Fig. 1-27. Luma watercolors.

Fig. 1-28. Shiva Shivair airbrush colors.

A Sampling of Media for Airbrush Work

The media listed here have been formulated by the manufacturers especially for the airbrush artist. They are all available in ready-to-use form. I have found these brands especially useful in my work.

Badger Air-Opaque. An opaque acrylic paint that dries to a water-resistant finish. Available in black, white, several shades of gray, and eighteen colors. Matte and glossy finish varnishes are also available.

Dr. P.H. Martins aniline dyes. Water-soluble pigments in a wide range of brilliant transparent colors. Available in regular and concentrated form. Their water solubility makes major corrections difficult. Dr. P.H. Martins produces an opaque white overpainting medium for such corrections. I have found however that its effect can be distracting on the original artwork although invisible in a reproduction of that artwork.

Holbein Aeroflash airbrush colors. Transparent and opaque versions of this acrylic paint are available.

Luma watercolors. Semi-transparent pigments in suspension. A very wide assortment of colors that remain water-soluble when dry. Variable lightfastness among the different colors makes their use best in commercial art intended primarily for reproduction. The manufacturer classifies colors by lightfastness.

Pelikan drawing inks. Prereduced for the airbrush artist. Available in a wide assortment of lightfast colors that are waterproof when dry.

Shiva Shivair watercolors. Available in transparent and opaque versions, both of which remain water soluble after application.

Winsor & Newton airbrush colors. Opaque acrylic paints that dry to a water-resistant finish. Contain some of the finest ground pigments available.

There is one potential drawback to using traditional watercolors and gouaches that come in tubes. They contain gum arabic as a binder. This will interact with the glue of many frisket films to form a sticky residue that is nearly impossible to clean off the artwork without damaging it. Be sure to test the colors and friskets for compatibility. It may be best to avoid using preglued, prepared friskets altogether when working with watercolor and gouache. Instead, use the nonadhesive vinyl and acetate frisket sheets.

One of the most versatile of media for all manner of art, fine and commercial, is acrylic polymer paint. It is water-based but is completely impermeable once dry. It dries very quickly to form a film of resilient, permanent plastic. The colors are brilliant and clear.

Fig. 1-29. Tube acrylics.

When diluted with enough water they are transparent, like watercolor, but when used in a thicker consistency, spread on with a palette knife or artist's brush, they are opaque like gouache.

Acrylics are my own preference. One characteristic of architectural illustration is that it is subject to modification—architects or clients may decide to alter the building design. When I am working with acrylic paints, these changes are easy to make. You can simply paint over or paint out without fear of any bleed-through from the layer below. And if you have an accident, such as spilling a filled color cup onto the middle of the drawing, the spill can be removed with a quick wipe of an absorbent lint-free tissue or cloth. A visible residue may remain on the plastic layer of paint, but this is easily corrected without bleed-through.

This medium is not completely free of drawbacks, however. The very qualities that recommend it to the airbrush artist can also cause problems. Because it is quick-drying and waterproof, it forms deposits of plastic inside the airbrush that can be difficult to remove, especially from delicate double-action, internal-mix airbrushes. The manufacturers have formulated special cleaning solvents, but even with these, cleanup is tedious. Still, I find acrylics indispensable in my work. I try to offset the problem of cleanup by using the simpler single-action brushes as much as possible.

Also, when using acrylic paint with a regular brush instead of an airbrush—certain effects are better achieved this way—avoid applying heavy impastos of paint. Under some circumstances, frisket film must be removed before the acrylic dries completely, but very wet paper tears more easily than dry or damp paper. Impastos always mean very wet paper. Impastos also tend to cast little shadows across the paper and to be very glossy and reflective, making photographic reproduction difficult. Because architectural illustration is usually meant to be reproduced, impastos are to be avoided.

Whatever media you use, I recommend that you test it, perhaps by performing the warm-up exercises and creating the geometric shapes described in chapter 2. You can make adjustments to the solution, thinning with water or adding more color. This will also give you a chance to set the color flow and experiment with adjustments and control.

Grounds are the supports or surfaces to which paint is applied. With the airbrush you can use just about anything as a ground—metal, ceramic, glass, canvas, paper—almost

anything your imagination dreams up. In architectural illustration, however, many of these grounds are simply impractical. I strongly recommend using the best-quality illustration board you can afford (for example, a Strathmore board such as Crescent No. 110, which has a 100 percent rag surface). With high-quality boards, you are less likely to have the top layer of paper pull off when you remove a frisket. These boards also hold up better when you must use an air eraser, a not-uncommon event in architectural rendering. Because high-quality boards are white through all their layers, they are less likely to reflect damage from the erosion of the air eraser.

Fig. 1-30. *Original illustration: 611 Wilshire, Los Angeles, California.*

Fig.1-31. *The same illustration after the building was redesigned. With acrylics, only the building had to be redone, saving the client time and the cost of a completely new rendering.*

OTHER TOOLS AND SUPPLIES

General studio equipment for airbrush work is the same as for most illustration work. You will need an assortment of drafting tools: T-squares and straight edges; a variety of templates, French curves and triangles; stencil knives; masking tapes. Friskets are essential to architectural illustration. If you are making these purchases now, look for tools in versions specially made for airbrush work whenever possible.

There are also some special tools and supplies that apply only to airbrush work: air hoses, airbrush holders, and air erasers, for example. Protective masks, a respirator (if necessary), ventilating equipment, and other protective devices should also be part of every airbrush studio. In fact, in any artist's studio, safety when working with hazardous materials should be a prime consideration.

Safety Tips

Every artist should be aware that artists' materials can be hazardous to your health. To minimize the risk, you should take proper precautions when working with dangerous substances. Here are some guidelines for the safe use of the airbrush. For more detailed information, consult *Artist Beware* by Michael McCann (New York: Watson-Guptill, 1979) or *A Painter's Guide to the Safe Use of Materials* by Nancy Seeger (Chicago: School of the Art Institute of Chicago, 1982).

- Make certain your studio or workspace is well ventilated. You may need to install

fans and an exhaust system. Contaminated air should be drawn away from your face. You might also consider using an air purifier if the substances you work with are particularly hazardous.

- Always wear a mask when working with the airbrush. This will reduce the risk of inhaling air-borne pigment particles, solvents, or propellants.

- Wear gloves and a respirator when working with enamels. Also consider wearing a respirator rather than a mask if you have a lung condition that might be worsened by exposure to airborne particles—or even if you have healthy lungs.

- Be careful not to point the nozzle of the airbrush at your skin. Some airbrushes operate with enough pressure to penetrate the skin and actually inject paint or other material into you. This can be very dangerous. It might be wise to wear protective clothing.

- If you will be spending a great deal of time using an airbrush or air eraser, consider purchasing a special spray booth that both filters and vents the air containing airborne particles.

- Never eat or drink in the studio. Ingesting particles that have settled on your food or beverage can be just as dangerous as inhaling them.

- Read manufacturers' labels and instructions carefully. Paint manufacturers are now required to list on paint containers the toxicity of the ingredients used, such as cadmium.

- Research the toxicity of the materials you use in one of the books listed in this section or the bibliography. Being aware of the danger is the best way to avoid it.

• Contact the National Institute for Occupational Safety and Health (NIOSH; Robert A. Taft Laboratory, 476 Columbia Parkway, Cincinnati, OH 45226) for their recommendations on safety and protective gear for airbrush work.

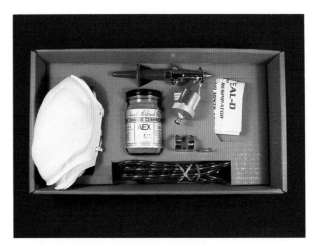

Fig. 1-32. Paasche AEC air eraser kit.

Air hoses are sold separately from the airbrush. The kind of air hose can affect the operation of the airbrush. Braided air hoses, for example, combine well with the heavier airbrushes; the extra weight of the brush counteracts the drag of the hose. Thin, plastic air hoses, on the other hand, are best with light airbrushes.

Airbrush holders are useful adjuncts that are supplied by the manufacturer or sold separately. They can be affixed to the wall or your work table, wherever they can be handily reached.

Most airbrush artists consider an air eraser more an essential tool than an accessory. This special-purpose airbrush operates much like a small sandblasting gun. Aluminum oxide powder is shot through the nozzle onto the work surface, which is thus eroded. This tool is used in dental lab work and jewelry-making, for cleaning all manner of metal components and miniature castings, and for etching glass and other materials. In architectural renderings, you must be able to change inkwork either to correct mistakes or to reflect design changes. The air eraser does a neat job of this without changing the texture of the paper appreciably.

Air erasers operate at a starting pressure of 10 to 15 psi. For the paper and boards used in architectural illustration, a pressure of 20 to 25 psi is required. Be sure to keep both instrument and air supply absolutely dry, installing a moisture trap if necessary. Any moisture in the unit will cause the abrasive to clump and

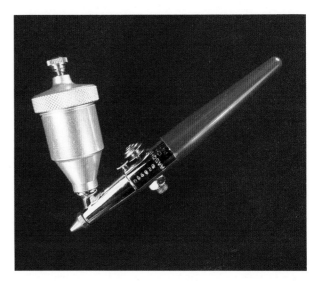

Fig. 1-33. Close-up view of the Paasche air eraser.

the unit to perform unevenly and intermittently, or to fail completely. It's also a good idea to shake the abrasive in the reservoir gently from time to time by pulsating the finger lever. This seems to assure even delivery. I use the Paasche AEC air eraser. It contains a carboloy tip insert that lasts longer than other tips and produces a more consistent fine-line technique.

Friskets are masks that cover part of the artwork while you work with the airbrush or other equipment. They allow you to protect an area from being sprayed. Friskets can be made from almost anything: erasing shields, French curves, templates, combs, torn blotting paper, loosely woven stiff fabrics, or whatever will give you the effect you are seeking. For architectural illustration, liquid frisket and frisket films are indispensable.

A Sampling of Friskets for Airbrush Work

In architectural illustration, liquid and preglued friskets are very useful. I have found the following brands to be of consistently good quality. This list is only a guide, and should not stop you from experimenting with other brands. New materials are continually being developed, and some materials suit some artists better than others. In making your selections, read the labels carefully. Some friskets must be removed quickly, otherwise they will become part of the artwork. Also avoid friskets with resin glues or very strong adhesives; these, too, can damage artwork beyond repair. They serve different purposes such as assembling collages.

Liquid Frisket
Art Masking Fluid by Winsor & Newton. A milky liquid containing ammonia, latex, and a yellow indicator dye, making it readily visible upon application.

Art Maskoid. A gray liquid with negligible staining properties.

Miskit by M. Grumbacher. A milky substance that contains an orange indicator dye, making it readily visible upon application. Dye settles in bottom of jar and must be stirred into solution; too much dye may stain white paper. To prevent such staining, if necessary, do not stir the jar, but use Miskit in its clear state.

Frisket Film
Graphix Prepared Frisket by Ohio Graphic Art Systems, Inc. This preglued frisket has a fairly strong adhesive, suitable for cold-press paper surfaces and colored mat boards. These grounds accept washes well and have a slightly rough texture. Graphix is easily burnished along the edges to counteract curling and strengthen adhesion. It rarely damages the artwork. It is also excellent for making removable collages or overlays. I have tried several of the other preglued frisket films, but cannot recommend them.

Liquid friskets are solutions of rubber and ammonia that are painted onto the support with a brush, pen, or ruling pen. As the liquid frisket dries, the ammonia evaporates and a protective film of latex is left. Later, when there is no longer any need for protecting this area of your work, the liquid frisket is simply peeled off. Please note, however, that liquid frisket cannot be used on existing artwork unless the art has been finished with acrylic, which is impervious to moisture. Check the finish before you accidentally ruin the art.

In applying liquid frisket, I have found that I get the best results by outlining irregular or intricate shapes with a crowquill pen dipped in the frisket. The large areas are then filled in with a brush. Use a ruling pen to cover long, thin lines. Make sure you use enough frisket;

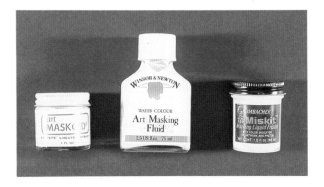

Fig. 1-34. Liquid friskets. Left to right: *Art Maskoid, Winsor & Newton's Art Masking Fluid, and Grumbacher's Miskit.*

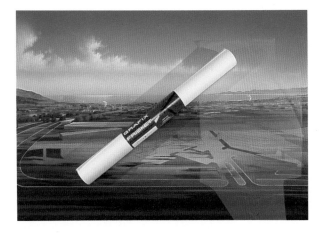

Fig. 1-35. Grafix prepared frisket.

this may mean more than one layer, depending on the tool you use and how experienced you are. Too thin an application will leave a porous coat that is easily penetrated by the medium you apply over it, thereby defeating the purpose of the frisket.

Frisket films will give the extremely clear, hard-edged separation between colors that is almost a trademark of architectural illustration. The films are either acetate or vinyl sheets. Some are clear, others frosted. Some are coated on one side with an adhesive; others are plain. Uncoated sheets rely on static electricity and atmospheric pressure to hold

their position on the artwork. Do not use uncoated acetate in rolls. It is impossible to get a piece cut from the roll to lie flat, making accurate frisketing very difficult.

Frisket films are cut with a razor knife right on the artwork you are protecting. With practice, you can cut the frisket without using too much pressure and damaging the paper below. If you inadvertently cut the paper when you are cutting the frisket, the paper will probably peel along the cut when you attempt to remove the frisket later. This is one reason you should use the best-quality 100 percent rag illustration boards for your work, with various textures depending on their intended use.

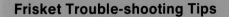

Frisket Trouble-shooting Tips

As helpful as friskets can be in creating architectural illustrations, they also have certain drawbacks. Here are some tips for offsetting or resolving these problems.

- However careful or practiced you are, there will still be times when you will cut into your artwork as you outline areas with the razor knife. I've done it myself. You can repair the damage by lifting off the frisket very carefully and cementing the cut paper back into place with a little bit of matte acrylic varnish. Use a clean, lint-free absorbent cloth or paper to dab away the excess.

- Occasionally you will want to use a regular brush instead of an airbrush to apply acrylic paint to your artwork. When you do, if you are also using a frisket, be sure to remove the frisket before the paint layer dries completely. Instead of airbrush dots of acrylic paint, there will be a continuous plastic film over both artwork and frisket once the brushed-on paint dries. Attempting to remove the frisket could result in tears in the paint film and damage to the artwork.

- Frisket films are temperature-sensitive and will bubble up from the surface of the artwork when heated. Prevent bubbling of frisket film once it's in place by keeping it cool. Do not rest your warm hand on the surface for long. Do not position a hot light bulb too near the frisket surface.

- If you get bubbles under the film as you are spreading the frisket, it is best to remove the frisket and start over. If this is impossible, puncture the frisket with the point of the razor knife and carefully squeeze out the air. To prevent seepage through this tiny hole, cover it with a small patch of frisket film.

- Curling of the edges of the frisket film is a frequent problem, despite manufacturers assurances to the contrary. Temperature changes, moisture, and poor handling of the airbrush are all contributing factors. Careful burnishing of the edge with a fingernail or burnishing tool will strengthen the adhesion and help prevent curling.

- To prevent curling on very delicate surfaces or highly detailed work where damage would be disastrous, do not burnish the edge of the frisket. The extra pressure might harm the surface. Instead, apply color in several very thin coats. The particles of color in a thin coat are almost dry when they reach the surface of the artwork and therefore less likely to cause curling.

- To avoid tearing your artwork, make certain that the medium you applied is completely dry before attempting to remove the frisket (except in the case of brushed-on acrylic, noted below). Wet paper fibers are weak and will tear easily.

- Protect your brushes when using them to spread on liquid frisket. Prepare a mixture of fairly thick white soap and water. Coat the hairs of a clean brush with this before dipping it into the frisket. The soap keeps rubbery deposits of frisket from forming on the brush. Even with the protection, however, expect brushes to wear out fairly quickly.

- To speed up drying time, use a hairdryer on liquid frisket.

Whether you use a preglued or plain frisket film depends upon the kind of ground you use. To cover very smooth paper, such as hot-pressed paper boards and photographs, use an uncoated or very low tack frisket film. For paper with texture, such as cold-pressed watercolor paper mounted on boards, a preglued frisket is best. Otherwise spray will seep under the frisket at the edges, following the irregularities of the paper surface. Even when applying a preglued frisket to such a surface, make certain that you burnish the edges to strengthen the seal and prevent seepage.

Because the preglued friskets can be expensive, if you have a large area to cover, use a combination of uncoated and preglued friskets. Cover the major portion of the area with the uncoated, water-resistant sheet. It need not be acetate; use less-expensive tracing paper, for example. Next, overlap this sheet with a strip of preglued frisket along the edge. Cut the preglued frisket to conform exactly to the edge of the area being protected. Check to make sure the frisket is well sealed along the edges, and fire away with your airbrush. If the shapes you are protecting are extremely intricate and cutting a frisket film would be awkward at best, use a combination of liquid frisket and frisket film.

Friskets are most often used to establish hard edges. However, I also use them for soft-edged effects: shadows on cylindrical and curvilinear subjects; window reflections; reflections in the water; or sky-scapes. These all require soft edges or blends from sharp linear separation to soft, rounded outlines. To achieve these effects with a frisket means progressively removing the frisket as you spray. (The technique is given in the exercises in chapter 2.)

Frisket films are also useful in creating removable collages or overlays. In architectural illustration, alterations to the design are practically a given. If there is one feature such as an awning over a doorway that is likely to be moved or modified, or if there is landscaping that will be added later, make a frisket overlay of this element that can then be moved easily from place to place on the paper

Fig. 1-37. Before you apply color, make sure the frisket is completely dry. Here, I have begun to airbrush a simple scene over the frisket.

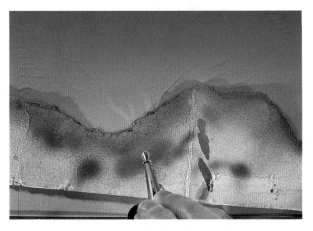

Fig. 1-38. Torn blotting paper can be used to create a separation between the sky and hills.

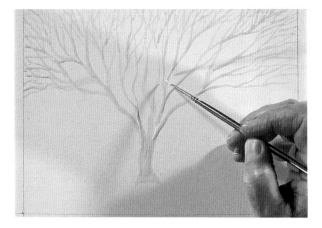

Fig.1-36. Intricate shapes that would be awkward and time-consuming to cut can be protected with liquid friskit. Apply liquid frisket with a small, fine brush and make sure there are no gaps of color to seep through. Avoid creating puddles of frisket; their dry surfaces can be misleading, covering a moist interior.

Fig. 1-39. The finished simple landscape before the liquid frisket is removed.

Fig.1-40. *Before removing the frisket, make sure everything is dry, including the support. Moisture softens the paper being worked on, and removing the frisket too soon will loosen the moist top layer of paper.*

Fig. 1-41. *Dried liquid frisket becomes a rubber film that is easy to pull off.*

Fig. 1-42. *The finished tree.*

or added later. For example, a completed building may eventually have a large tree planted in front of it, but you are not sure where it will be placed. If you take a chance and position it permanently as part of your artwork, you may have to redo the entire passage later when you discover that the position has changed. Instead, if you make a frisket of the tree, it can be positioned and repositioned until everyone is satisfied. Then the frisket itself can be varnished in place if time does not allow for painting it in. I like to keep a frisket file of such bits and pieces—trees, shrubbery, people, cars, and similar subjects. They save much time in visualizing the position of such details on a finished illustration.

As this chapter has shown, equipment in the airbrush studio is similar to that in any drafting studio, with the addition of things specially designed for airbrush use. While I don't believe in running out and buying everything at once, especially if you are in the early days of airbrush work, the tools and supplies described above are ones I consider essential to architectural illustration with the airbrush. With them, you will be able to perform the exercises and duplicate the demonstrations in the pages that follow.

2

LEARNING THE TECHNIQUE
Basic Exercises

As with any acquired skill, airbrushing demands practice if you are to become well versed in its use. It takes practice, for example, to master the smooth coordinated movements of the arm, wrist, and index finger that are essential to airbrush work. While you may already have attained good control over your airbrush, it is useful to go back to the basics now and then. You might want to do the warm-up exercises and render the basic solid geometric forms whenever you break in a new airbrush. It's a little like taking a new car out for a spin or putting a thoroughbred through its paces.

TIPS FOR OPERATING THE AIRBRUSH

Rather than give a step-by-step lesson in the basics of handling an airbrush, I will share with you some of the tips I have followed or developed over the years.

Controlling air flow. Air flow over the spray tip, the distance from spray tip to work surface, and the rate of color flow are the three basic variables in airbrush work. Control of these three elements is essential to success with the airbrush. Color flow can be preset, and distance is easily established (if not so easily maintained). I have developed my own somewhat unorthodox methods to control air flow. They are based on my experience with a single-action diffuser, the Paasche Model H, but the same technique can be used successfully with double-action airbrushes.

Set the pressure regulator on the compressor or gas cylinder at 30 to 35 psi and use the air valve on the airbrush for all intermediate pressures. Make your adjustments to the air-valve setting by using the thumb and middle finger to counteract the index finger's downward force on the air-valve lever. This eliminates the problems caused by a twitchy index finger or a recalcitrant air-valve mechanism.

Maintaining continuity. One inevitable problem is losing the momentum in the middle of a project because you have to change colors, spray tips, needles, or to make some other adjustment to your equipment. This problem is easily solved by using more than one airbrush simultaneously. This is especially useful when you are using two colors in a small area—to render precast concrete, for example, where a base color will be covered with a contrasting spatter coat to represent the aggregate. The operation is quick enough to keep the color in either airbrush from drying and will give continuity to the work.

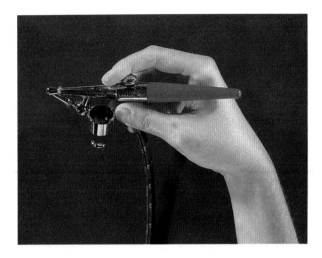

Fig. 2-1. *The correct way to operate an airbrush.*

Fig. 2-2. *The thumb and middle finger counteract the downward push of an inexperienced index finger, making the airbrush more controllable and the spray constant.*

Stopping to empty, clean, and refill a single airbrush over and over again is tedious, not to say time-consuming.

Another tip for maintaining continuity is putting the assembly line into practice when you have several projects of similar scope underway. Line them up and do all the sky-scapes at once—background, then clouds—followed by all the buildings, then all the landscapes. The nature of the project will suggest the order and content of assembly.

Softening and blending edges. Soft edges where shadow blends into lighted areas can be made by using a frisket. Attach the frisket to the ground, securing it at either end of the edge so that it resembles an inchworm or a bridge. Spray along the edge, keeping the airbrush at a fixed distance from the frisket. This will mean arcing away from the surface of your work. Try a variation of this by ignoring the curve of the frisket and keeping the airbrush a fixed distance from the ground instead.

To get a blend from direct contact separation to graduated tone, use the same strip keeping one end aloft with your free hand. The frisket assumes a sort of hyperbola shape when viewed from the side. Spray along the contact edge, working past the separation.

WARM-UP EXERCISES

If you are using a brand new airbrush, begin by checking its operation. Fill the color cup with plain water. Set the appropriate air pressure on your air supply. In most cases, this will be about 20 to 30 psi. Hold the airbrush over a dark background, and release a spray of water. Run the airbrush through the full range of its spray and observe it as you do. This will give you a feel for the new brush. You will be able to see that the spray is even, the needle straight, and so on.

Once you are satisfied, empty the color cup and reload with medium. Black on white paper, or white on black paper, is best for warm-ups. These exercises give you practice in dots, lines, and tones. They not only familiarize you with the range of a new airbrush, but help teach you control over it.

Materials

All of the exercises in this chapter were performed with the following tools. You can substitute similar makes and models for brands listed below. You will not need everything for every exercise.

Airbrush: Paasche Model H, single-action diffuser.

Media: Dr. P.H. Martins black for dots and lines, Badger Air-Opaque liquid acrylics, and tube acrylics from various manufacturers. Try to select media that are easy to clean from the airbrush. It is tedious to spend more time than you must cleaning the airbrush.

Ground: Crescent No. 110 illustration board; Crescent colored mat board.

Friskets: Graphix preglued film, blotting paper, paper towels, scrap paper, tracing paper, cardboard.

Other supplies: Practice boards (scraps from old boards), clear plastic templates, triangles, straight edge, compass, cutting compass, X-acto knife, ruling pen, pencil.

1. Making Dots (Fig. 2-3)

With a pencil make several lines of dots, spaced about a half-inch apart. Pointing the airbrush at the first dot in the first line, apply air and gradually open the spray tip. Adjust the airbrush-to-surface distance until you create a fuzzy little dot on the mark. Continue to make these dots until you become fairly proficient in producing dots of similar size.

For variety, space the dots farther apart and make larger dots. This will demonstrate the variables resulting from holding the airbrush at different distances from the work surface. Imagine the spray pattern as a cone. The tip of the cone is at the tip of the airbrush; the base, on the surface of the paper. The farther the airbrush from the work surface, the larger the base circle. If the color flow is preset, the farther the airbrush from the work surface, the thinner the application of medium. Conversely, the closer the airbrush, the smaller and denser (darker) the circle.

2. Making Lines (Fig. 2-4)

Hold the airbrush very close to the surface of the paper, maintaining an equal distance from the beginning to end of each stroke. Each line must be made in one smooth motion. It can be difficult to make short lines that end cleanly. One good tip is to use a frisket to cut off the line where you want. A mask as simple as a piece of paper will be sufficient. Continue making lines until you feel comfortable with the airbrush. For variation, make wider lines by widening the distance between paper and airbrush tip.

Fig. 2-4.

Fig. 2-3.

3. Producing Tone (Figs. 2-5 through 2-9)

In this exercise you will practice simple tonal effects. For it, I have decided to use a dark sheet of paper and load the airbrush with Badger's Air-Opaque white. The end result is an imaginary, atmospheric night sky.

Fig. 2-5. Using a piece of blotter as a frisket, tear out an irregular shape and position it against the ground. With a smooth motion, sweep the airbrush over the frisket, holding it firmly in place and maintaining the same finger position over the air valve and the same distance from the paper. (It is a good idea to establish the spray pattern on a piece of scrap paper first.) You will have to make several passes over a large area. To vary the tone, feather the spray in the lighter areas and make even more passes over dark areas.

Fig. 2-6. Study the effect you have just created in preparation for the next step.

Fig. 2-7. Position a circle template against the dark paper and cover the other areas with friskets.

Fig. 2-8. The two-dimensional circles have been sprayed and shaded to create spheres (see *Solid Geometric Forms,* following).

Fig. 2-9. To produce heavy textures, lower the air pressure either on the air-supply source if it has a regulator, or on the airbrush itself by depressing the air valve as little as possible. Then, while applying air, open the spray tip orifice very slowly. The quality of the tone produced will become coarser this way. The variables are wide-ranging: size of the airbrush, distance from the paper, consistency of the paint, diameter of the spray-tip opening, amount of air pressure. All will determine the coarseness and kind of spatter effect you can achieve. And all of these will affect the textures you create.

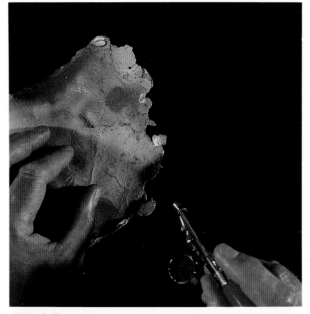

Fig. 2-5.

Fig. 2-6.

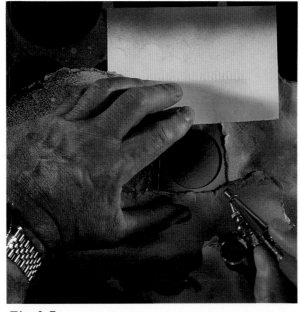

Fig. 2-7.

Fig. 2-9.

Fig. 2-8.

EXERCISES IN SOLID GEOMETRIC FORMS

The basic three-dimensional forms are the cube, cone, and sphere. In architecture, the cylinder is also a basic shape. In the exercises that follow you will practice making these three shapes in solid form, and will be encouraged to manipulate them in several variations that are the basis of building types.

Rendering a three-dimensional object requires an understanding of the principles of light and shadow. Reflected light will glance off planes that are in shade, and shadows cast by the object will be darker than the planes in shade. The ground plane and sky will reflect light off surfaces in open shade. Observe the light patterns on a building, especially a glass one, to see this and the other principles at work.

To produce the solid forms in these exercises, the steps are essentially the same. First airbrush the cast shadows; second, the side in shade; third, the side in direct light.

1. The Cube (Figs. 2-10 through 2-20).

Fig. 2-10. First draw a cube on your illustration board, using pencil. Decide on the location of the light source—in the example shown, it is to the right. Draw in the cast shadow, in this case, to the left. Cover the drawing with a piece of preglued frisket. (For photographic clarity only, the lines of the drawing were traced onto the frisket with a ruling pen.) Make sure that there is a wide margin of frisket around the drawing. To save frisket, you can use a combination of preglued frisket and tracing paper or another mask.

Fig. 2-11. With an X-acto knife, trace the lines of the cube and its cast shadow, scoring through the frisket but not into the surface of the paper. Keep the pressure even.

Fig. 2-10.

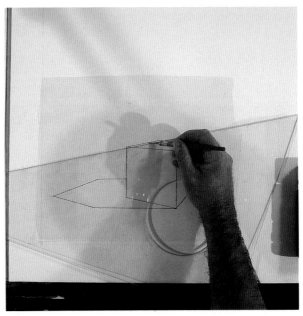

Fig. 2-11.

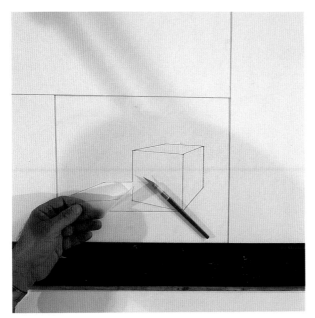

Fig. 2-12.

Fig. 2-13.

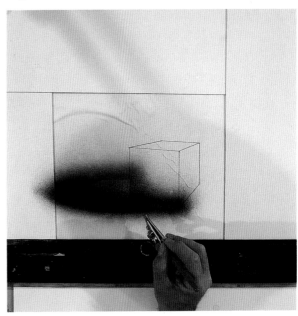

Fig. 2-14.

Fig. 2-12. Whether you use a combination frisket or just a preglued one, cover the area beyond it, to protect it from spray. Peel off the frisket from the cast shadow area.

Fig. 2-13. Load your airbrush with black, and make a few test sprays on a paper towel.

Fig. 2-14. Smoothly and evenly spray the cast shadow area. Rest your hand on a separate support to protect the preglued frisket from direct contact with the warmth of your hand, which may cause bubbling. In the picture I am using a wide straight edge for this purpose.

Fig. 2-15. Continue spraying. This will be the darkest area in the finished drawing.

Fig. 2-16. Peel off the frisket from the plane on the cube that is in shadow.

Fig. 2-17. Spray that side, but create a darker tone, almost as dark as the cast shadow, in the corner and side nearest the viewer—in this case, the upper right.

Fig. 2-18. Remove the frisket from the top of the cube and spray. In this case the tone should be a little darker on the right of this plane.

Fig. 2-19. Remove the frisket from the right side of the cube. This is the side in direct light. It will be the lightest area on the object. Give it a light spray with the airbrush, feathering the tone toward the back of the cube, making it darker toward the front, nearest the viewer.

Fig. 2-20. Remove the rest of the frisket and you have the finished cube.

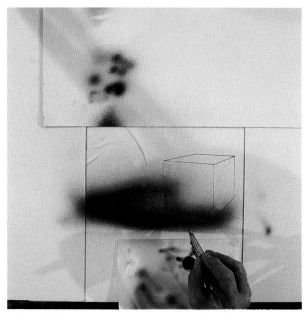

Fig. 2-15.

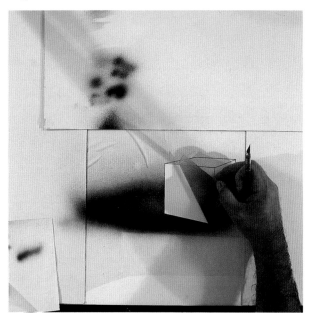

Fig. 2-16.

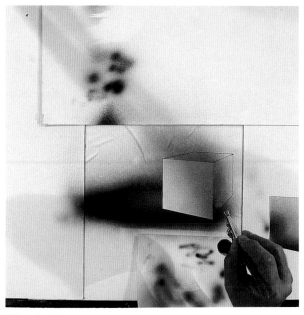

Fig. 2-17.

Fig. 2-19.

Fig. 2-18.

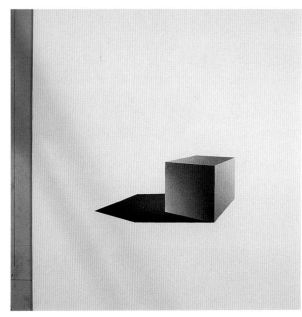

Fig. 2-20.

2. Variations on the Cube (Figs. 2-21 through 2-26).

In this exercise, you will begin to experiment with creating a building form in space. As you can see, it is based on the form of the cube and follows the same principles and procedures of light and shadow.

Fig. 2-21. Prepare the drawing and frisket just as you did in the cube exercise. Again, study the sketch and decide where the cast shadows will fall. In this case, the light is coming from the right and above and the building shape is uneven, so it will cast one shadow on the ground and another on itself. This often happens with architectural forms. Peel the frisket from the two cast shadows.

Fig. 2-22. Airbrush these areas until you have a very dark even tone.

Fig. 2-23. Peel and spray the underside of the overhang. This will be in full shade and will be the next darkest area. Feather the edge that meets the dark shadow on the building plane. Repeat this with the left plane of the building, which should be about as dark as the area just sprayed. The part nearest the viewer should be slightly darker than that farthest away.

Fig. 2-24. Peel and spray the final two planes, both of which are in direct light and will be the lightest areas on the building surface.

Fig. 2-25. Peel all the remaining frisket, and you have the finished building.

Fig. 2-26. As an additional effect, re-cover the drawing with frisket and cut an opening the exact shape of the building, but not the shadow cast on the ground. Spray this area with a wash of a warm color such as yellow ochre. The feeling is quite different from the black-and-white object in space.

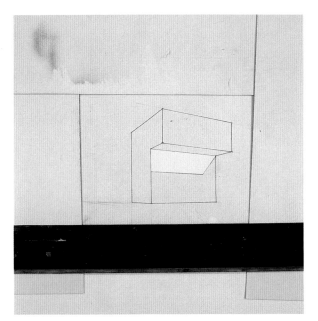

Fig. 2-21.

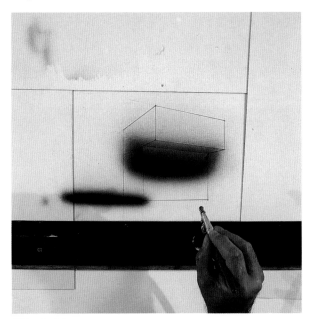

Fig. 2-22.

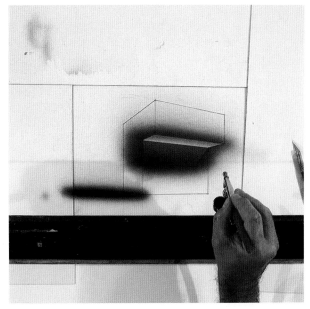

Fig. 2-23.

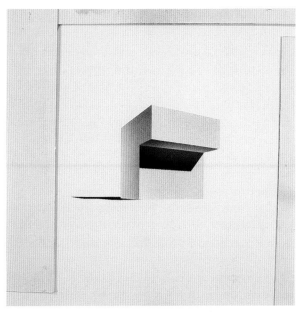

Fig. 2-25.

Fig. 2-24.

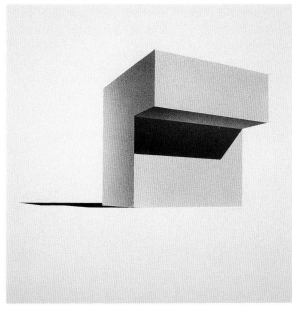

Fig. 2-26.

3. The Cylinder (Figs. 2-27 through 2-30)

The steps in this exercise are very much like
those taken to render a cube. If you have any
doubt, go back to figures 2-10 through 2-22
and review those steps.

Fig. 2-27. Prepare the drawing and frisket
with pencil, ruling pen, and X-acto knife.

Fig. 2-28. Peel the frisket from the shadow
and spray it an even, dark color, the darkest
in the drawing.

Fig. 2-29. Peel the frisket from the vertical
plane of the cylinder, leaving the top, the horizontal plane, covered. Spray up and down
with even strokes, aiming to achieve three
gradations of tone: darkest, to the left where
the cylinder is in deepest shade; lightest, in
the middle right, where the cylinder faces the
light source; medium tone, to the right where
the cylinder begins to fall in shadow again.
This gradation will give a nice rounded form
to the cylinder.

Fig. 2-30. The finished cylinder. The frisket
from the top of the cylinder has been peeled
away and it has been given a light, almost
even spray of color.

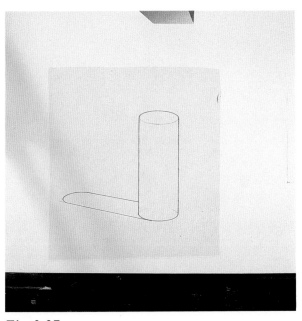

Fig. 2-27.

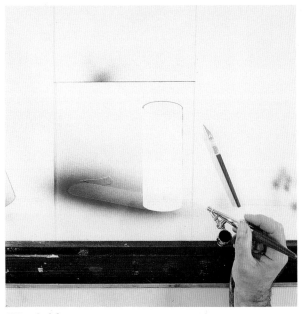

Fig. 2-28.

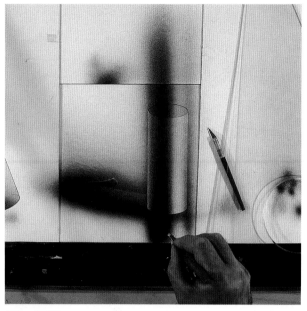

Fig. 2-29.

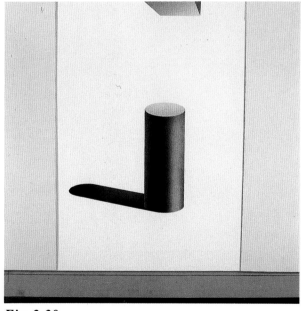

Fig. 2-30.

4. Variation on a Cylinder (Figs. 2-31 through 2-34)

Anyone who has ever seen the Guggenheim Museum in New York City will understand that architects often make use of the cylinder in their work. Inside and out, Frank Lloyd Wright based his design on cylinder and spiral. In this exercise, you will experiment with rendering a variation on this form.

Fig. 2-31. Draw a three-dimensional section of a cylinder and its cast shadow. Prepare the frisket. You will have six pieces of frisket to peel off and spray. The first, as in every exercise, is that covering the shadow. Spray this area to establish your most even, darkest tone.

Fig. 2-32. Next peel away the piece of frisket covering the area of the cylinder in deepest shadow. Spray, feathering the tone to be lightest where the form begins to bend around back.

Fig. 2-33. The curved inner face is next. This will have a dark area where it is shading itself and will gradually become lighter as it moves into direct light.

Fig. 2-34. The two forward end planes are worked on next, and finally the horizontal top plane (neither step is shown). The finished form is an interesting lesson in form and tone.

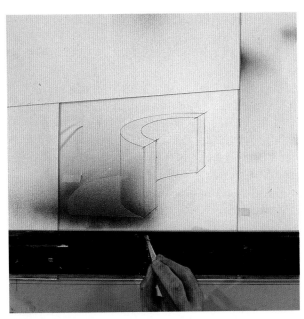

Fig. 2-31.

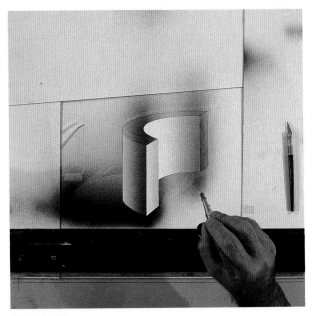

Fig. 2-33.

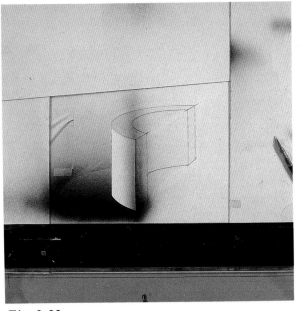

Fig. 2-32.

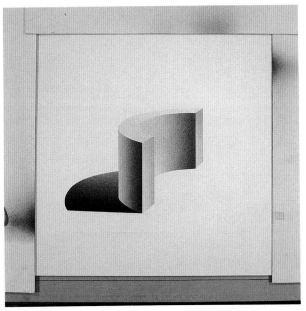

Fig. 2-34.

5. The Sphere (Figs. 2-35 through 2-38)

Rendering a sphere may have the fewest steps, but in some ways it is the trickiest form to do well. How confidently you handle the airbrush, how steady you are, how keen your perceptions of form, light, and shadow will all determine how successful the finished shape is. The steps themselves are no different from those in making a cube.

Fig. 2-35. With a compass or cirlce template trace a circle on your board. Sketch in the cast shadow; note that the shadow of a sphere begins directly under it. Cover the drawing with preglued frisket and cut around it with a cutting compass or X-acto knife. Peel the frisket from the cast shadow.

Fig. 2-36. After spraying in an even dark tone over the cast shadow, peel the frisket off the circle.

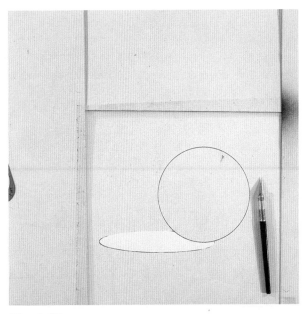

Fig. 2-35.

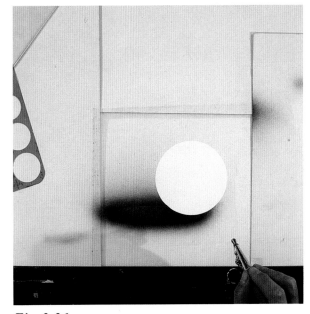

Fig. 2-36.

Fig. 2-37. To give the illusion of solid roundness, spray with a circular motion, feathering from the edge nearest the cast shadow, starting at the top and working in a C shape around that edge of the circle. The lightest area should be a small circular area facing the light source.

Fig. 2-38. Remove all remaining frisket. It may take a few attempts at rendering this form before you are satisfied with it.

Fig. 2-37.

Fig. 2-38.

6. Variation on a Sphere (Figs. 2-39 and 2-40)

Warm and cool colors can create different effects when applied to solid forms. Use warm colors in lighted areas, cool colors in shadows, as demonstrated by this exercise. Study the works of pointillist painters and you will see that they used this system in their works.

Fig. 2-39. Re-cover the sphere just rendered with a new frisket. Cut and peel just the sphere, leaving the cast shadow covered. Choose a pale, cool, bluish tint. For this demonstration, my choice was a mixture of white and powder blue. Spray this lightly in the shadow area of the sphere.

Fig. 2-40. On the opposite side, where the light is hitting the sphere, spray a hint of a warm color. My choice was a mixture of naples yellow, ochre, and white.

These, then, are the basics: dot, line, tone; cube, cylinder, sphere. Much of architectural illustration is based on these simple forms and techniques. Practice and master them and you are well on your way to producing fine work.

Fig. 2-39.

Fig. 2-40.

3

ARCHITECTURAL APPLICATIONS
Advanced Exercises

For architectural application, you must be able to render surfaces of different materials in three dimensions. The basics for this are precast concrete, stucco, brick, and marble—most others will be variations of these four textures. A series of exercises will help you understand surface treatments and their applications to architecture. For each of the exercises you will need many of the same materials listed at the beginning of chapter 2, as well as a palette of colors listed on the following page.

BASIC SURFACE TREATMENTS

These exercises give you some of the basic vocabulary of architectural illustration.

Exercise 1: Precast Concrete and Stucco

This is a quick exercise in creating the look of precast concrete and stucco. (Note: when you have completed this exercise, save the paint mixes, to use in a later exercise.)

Palette: unbleached titanium, raw siena, white, black, flesh, sepia, and powder blue.

Fig. 3-1. Start just as you have in earlier exercises. Draw two contiguous rectangles—these will be the sides of your "building," one side in shade, the other in light. You may either draw your outlines with a pencil and lay down a preglued frisket, or cover the work surface with a preglued frisket and draw your outlines onto the frisket with a pencil or ruling pen. Then trace the outlines again with an X-acto knife. Peel away the frisket from the shaded side and spray on the basic color, in this case unbleached titanium, white, and raw siena.

Fig. 3-2. Darken this same area with a harmonious shade, in this case, a mixture of raw umber and a minute bit of black. To achieve a realistic texture, reduce the air pressure, open the spray tip about a three-quarter turn, and spray the shaded area lightly, holding the airbrush a bit farther back than previously. Try a test pattern on scrap board first, to be sure that you are getting the right splatter effect.

Fig. 3-1.

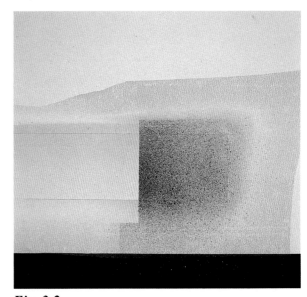

Fig. 3-2.

Fig. 3-3. Repeat the same two steps on the sunny side, spraying less base coat and less splatter texture.

Fig. 3-4. Indicate the joints with a ruling pen.

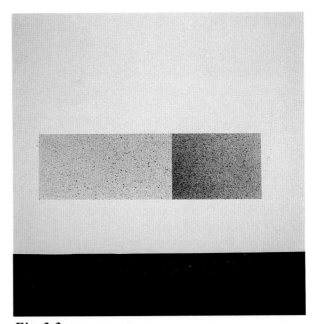

Fig. 3-3.

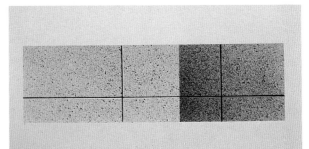

Fig. 3-4.

Exercise 2: Brick

The object here is a two-dimensional brick wall. It is a bit more complicated than precast concrete or stucco until you break it down into manageable steps. First, prepare your illustration board by drawing a rectangle, covering it with frisket, and cutting out a window that exactly fits the rectangle. (Note: when you have completed this exercise, save the finished drawing and the color mixes, to use in a later exercise.)

Palette: burnt umber, cadmium yellow medium, payne's gray, raw siena, red oxide, white, flesh, sepia, and black.

Fig. 3-5. Set the airbrush to deliver a coarse spray and apply the base color—in this case, a mixture of red oxide, raw siena, burnt umber, and cadmium yellow medium.

Fig. 3-6. To the leftover base color, add white and flesh tone. Reduce pressure and open the nozzle (as in exercise 1), and spray a splattering of this color to give the effect of aggregate.

Fig. 3-5.

Fig. 3-6.

Fig. 3-7. For dark aggregate, mix payne's gray and burnt umber and apply another splatter coat.

Fig. 3-8. Once this paint has dried, rule in the mortar joints using a rule pen and white and raw siena. Then rule in the shadow lines with a mixture of burnt umber, black, and a touch of flesh on the appropriate two sides of each brick.

Fig. 3-9. If the bricks have a range, that is, some are darker than others, make a brick-size movable frisket using two pieces of uncoated stock (cardboard) as shown here. Move it around the wall and randomly darken some bricks with the dark-aggregate tone and highlight others with the light-aggregate tone.

Fig. 3-10. The finished wall.

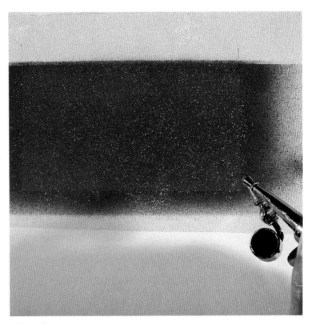

Fig. 3-7.

Fig. 3-8.

Fig. 3-9.

Fig. 3-10.

Exercise 3: Marble

Marble is the most demanding of these three basic exercises. You must have some expertise in doing dots, lines, tones, and textures. Be sure to have some scrap paper or board handy to test colors and technique. Begin by sketching and frisketing the outline of a large, vertical rectangle.

Palette: black, cadmium red, payne's gray, raw siena, raw umber, unbleached titanium, and white.

Fig. 3-11. Apply a base coat of color at high pressure. The color in this case is a mixture of unbleached titanium, white, and raw siena.

Fig. 3-12. Using the line technique described in the warm-up exercises section at the beginning of this chapter, establish a lacework pattern of veins. Use individual applications of tints of raw umber, raw siena, white, unbleached titanium, and payne's gray. Notice the position of the airbrush in this picture. The Paasche Model H spray-tip casting surrounds the needle assembly. Resting this casting on the work surface helps to maintain an equal distance between the airbrush and the work surface and assures the production of lines of equal width.

Fig. 3-13. Tear a few pieces of blotter and use them together to create wider veins with tints of one or two of the colors above. I chose a tint of payne's gray for this example.

Fig. 3-14. The last step in the exercise is giving the marble a final splatter coat in a dark color—in this case, raw umber—to mimic the texture of some marbles. Reduce air pressure and open the nozzle orifice to get this splatter effect.

Fig. 3-11.

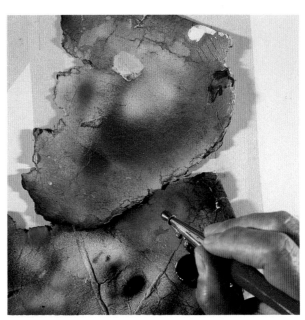

Fig. 3-13.

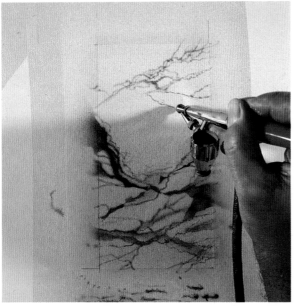

Fig. 3-12.

Fig. 3-14.

Fig. 3-15. This is another example of marble. It was created in a slightly different way from the step-by-step procedure just described. Pure black was used as the base coat. A mixture of unbleached titanium, white, and a tiny bit of cadmium red was used for the veining. This mixture was puddled onto the frisket at the edge of the art, just where I wanted a large vein to begin. With air pressure only, the airbrush was directed at the puddle and used to blow the paint across the surface to create the intricate, lacy veining. Touching the rivulets of wet paint with blotting paper changed the intensity of color, emphasizing a mottled effect. I repeated the puddle-and-vein technique many times to create this surface.

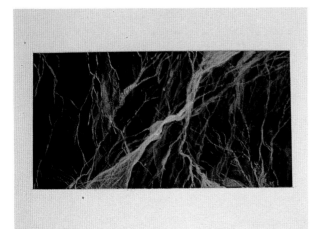

Fig. 3-15.

THREE-DIMENSIONAL SURFACE TREATMENTS

It's all very well to be able to make a drawing of a flat panel of marble or a brick wall, but building surfaces are broken with doors, windows, archways, or other architectural details. You must be able, therefore, to show the basic materials convincingly in a variety of configurations.

Exercise 1: Building Detail

Two approaches to architectural detail will be given. In the first, you will proceed from cast shadow, to shade, to light, to base coat. In exercise 2 the order is reversed. The first way is quicker, but produces a softer result. This may be just the effect you want at times. The second way may be more time consuming, but the results are very crisp.

Palette: Atelier raw siena; Badger Air Opaque black, flesh, powder blue, sepia, white; Shiva unbleached titanium.

Fig. 3-16. Sketch a three-dimensional mockup of a building detail such as the one shown here. Decide on the location of the light source and sketch in the appropriate shadows cast on the building. Prepare a frisket as you have for previous exercises.

Fig. 3-17. Peel and spray the shaded areas starting with the cast shadows. Use a mixture of sepia and black, and apply in a coarse spray. You will be working from dark to light in the following order.

Fig. 3-18. Peel and spray the shaded area on the soffit.

Fig. 3-19. Peel and spray areas of open shade (right).

Fig. 3-20. Peel and spray the sunny area farthest from the viewer.

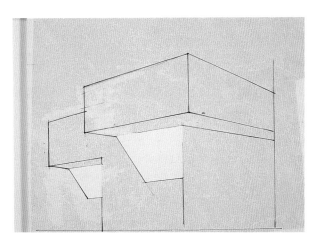

Fig. 3-16.

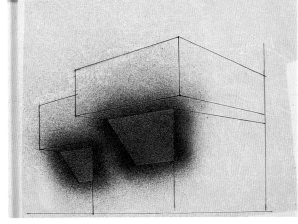

Fig. 3-17.

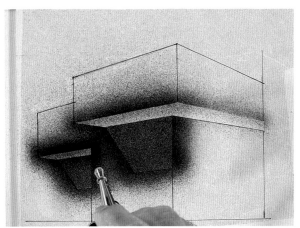

Fig. 3-18.

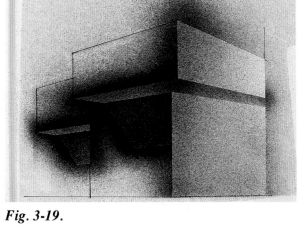

Fig. 3-19.

Fig. 3-20.

Fig. 3-21. Finally, peel and spray the remaining surfaces in successive steps, completing the sunny area nearest the viewer last. This will be the lightest tone in the building, which is now essentially complete.

Fig. 3-22. As a finishing touch spray a mixture of titanium, raw siena, and white lightly over the entire surface. Then spray a mixture of powder blue and white into the upper right-hand corner. Note how these additional coats have softened the effects of light and shade.

Fig. 3-23. The finished drawing, friskets removed.

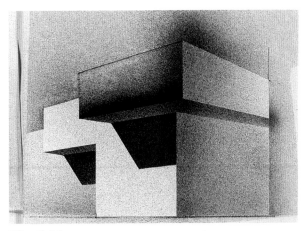

Fig. 3-21.

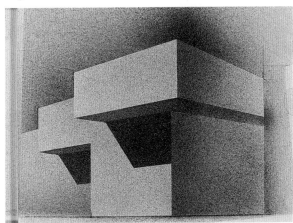

Fig. 3-22.

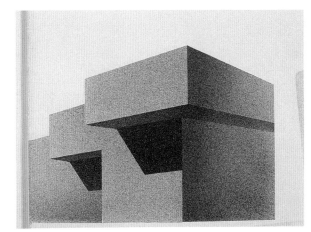

Fig. 3-23.

Exercise 2: Alternative Method—Light to Dark

In this exercise, the drawing of a precast concrete or stucco building is produced by spraying the lightest areas first, darkest areas last. A glass panel will give you an opportunity to begin to explore the rendering of this material.

Palette: Same as in exercise 1.

Fig. 3-24. Draw and frisket a building mockup. In this case the frisket should cover only the background area, leaving the entire building exposed.

Fig. 3-25. Spray on an even base coat of a mixture of titanium, raw siena, and white.

Fig. 3-26. Frisket and cut all outlines relating to shadows, the shaded side, and the soffit. These areas will be done in three steps, with one frisketing. Remove the cast shade and apply sepia and black in two separate steps. Repeat these steps on the soffit, leaving it a little lighter.

Fig. 3-27. Remove the frisket from the surfaces in open shade and airbrush in sepia and black.

Fig. 3-28. Remember the basic tenet: the farther from view, the lighter the subject is.

Fig. 3-29. The completed form, frisket removed.

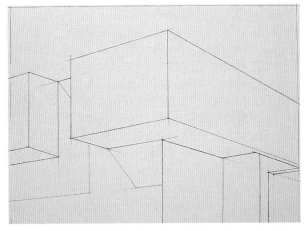

Fig. 3-24.

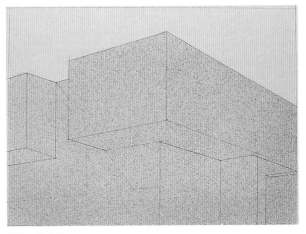

Fig. 3-25.

Fig. 3-26.

Fig. 3-28.

Fig. 3-27.

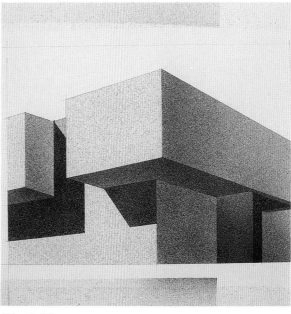

Fig. 3-29.

Fig. 3-30. The glass panel is finished, with powder blue and flesh used for the base coat and highlights, black for reflections and shading. In this instance, the wavy lines usually found in reflections have been dispensed with in favor of a clean, geometric look.

Fig. 3-31. Mullions are added with a ruling pen, using black, and a mix of powder blue and white is added for the highlights. The screed or construction joints are ruled in with a mixture of black and raw siena; the highlights are a mixture of flesh, raw siena, and white.

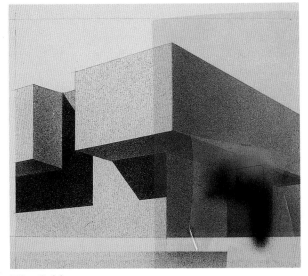

Fig. 3-30.

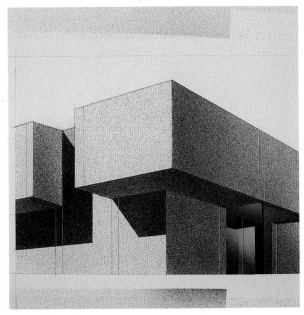

Fig. 3-31.

Exercise 3. Three-Dimensionality in Brick

For this exercise you will use the drawing of the brick wall, an early exercise in this chapter. While the end result is a fantasy in brick, the exercise will give you an idea of how light and shadow on brickwork give it the third dimension essential to architectural drawing.

Palette: Badger's flesh tone, burnt siena, and burnt umber.

Fig. 3-32. I first covered the drawing with a preglued frisket, into which I cut out a pattern of openings. In this view, using the mixture of burnt siena and burnt umber, I have begun spraying what will be a dark shadow area.

Fig. 3-33. I have peeled off the area of brick that will be casting the shadow just produced. Many buildings have such corner overhangs. This area has been darkened with a coarse but lighter application of the same mix of burnt siena and burnt umber. Immediately, three-dimensionality has been established.

Fig. 3-34. I have lightened the face of the new overhang with a mixture of Badger's flesh and burnt siena. This highlights the sunlit face of the overhang, to stand out from the rest of the facade. Using a piece of cardboard as a frisket, I sprayed a little burnt umber on the upper portion of the already shaded wall to make it recede somewhat. This approach can be used in rendering elevations of complicated buildings with walls meeting at angles greater than 90 degrees.

Fig. 3-32.

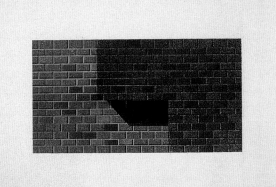

Fig. 3-33.

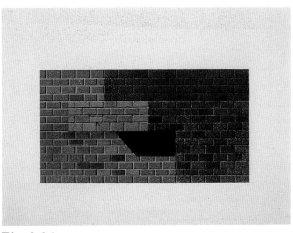

Fig. 3-34.

Exercise 4: Marble

Marble is a highly reflective surface. Because
it does not warp when installed, as glass does,
it reflects its surrounding without distortion.
Observe the surface reflections of marble in
the lobby of a large office building. Areas in
sun or bright light will appear to be less reflective than those in shade. In this exercise, you
will capture the look of marble and its reflective qualities. Before you begin, review the
step-by-step lesson in rendering a marble
plane given earlier in this chapter *(Basic Surface Treatments, Exercise 3: Marble)*. The
finished form is a freestanding block of marble, almost a pair of marble monoliths, if you
will.

Palette: Badger Air-Opaque aqua, black,
blue, flesh, powder blue, and white; Winsor &
Newton acrylic sap green (tube).

Fig. 3-35. Cover the entire layout with frisket. Cut the appropriate outlines, then
uncover the surfaces in shade. Begin working
on the reflection of the cast shadow on the
central recessed plane. For the base color, use
a smooth transparent spray of aqua, then sap
green. After the cast shadow develops a deep
color, coat the planes in open shade with a
lighter spray of transparent hue.

Fig. 3-36. Airbrush the veining and hints of
reflected objects with a mixture of black, sap
green, and aqua. Add highlights in the veining
with white, flesh, and powder blue.

Fig. 3-37. Replace the old frisket with a
fresh sheet of frisket. Begin working on the
sunlit surfaces, removing the frisket first from
the cast shadow only. To create the shadow,
use sap green and aqua mixed with black. Use
powder blue to create the hint of reflection; a
darker mixture of sap green, aqua, and black
to do the veining.

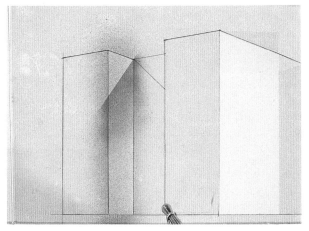

Fig. 3-35.

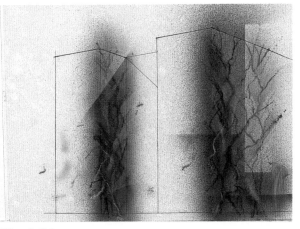

Fig. 3-36.

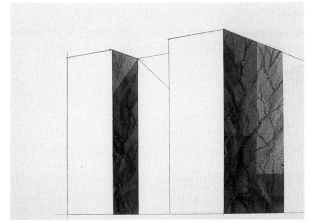

Fig. 3-37.

Fig. 3-38.

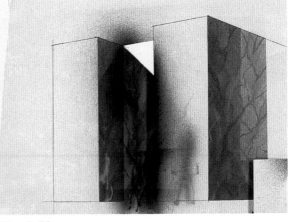

Fig. 3-39.

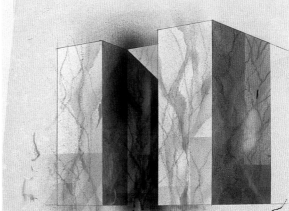

Fig. 3-40.

Fig. 3-38. Color the section shown with a coat of sap green, then aqua.

Fig. 3-39. The little triangular area is next. Breaking the "farther is lighter" rule, this sunlit surface is finished darker than the two major illuminated surfaces in front of it; thus, the separation will be more pronounced.

Fig. 3-40. The remaining two areas are rendered with very light smooth tones, sap green and flesh being the major colors. Slightly cooler and darker blues—aqua and powder blue—give a hint of reflection and the veining is added with a mix of black, sap green, and aqua. This example may be found on exterior surfaces and in atria that receive light directly from above.

Fig. 3-41. The finished illustration, frisket removed.

Fig. 3-41.

RENDERING IMPORTANT DETAILS

Complicated corner treatments, glass facades, and intricate sky-scapes are often met in architectural illustration. The following exercises will help you master the handling of these details.

Exercise 1: A Corner Window

Corner offices may seem quite complicated to render as seen from the outside until broken down into their components, all of which are also components of earlier exercises. In the example shown, the corner is based on a frequently used design: recessed glass with butt joints in a building of warm, reddish-brown precast concrete with heavy, exposed aggregate.

Palette: Badger Air-Opaque black, brown, flesh, white, powder blue, and varnish.

Fig. 3-42. Draw the mockup of a typical corner detail.

Fig. 3-43. Cover the drawing with preglued frisket, then cut the frisket along the outline of surfaces in the sun and in indirect or open shade. Assume that the sun is positioned at the upper left, and leave the side in shade exposed. Set the air pressure at 35 psi and open the spray tip about two turns.

Fig. 3-44. Start by applying a coarse spray of brown. Modulate the air pressure as needed.

Fig. 3-45. Using the same approach, apply a coarse spray of flesh color to soften the brown texture.

Fig. 3-46. Add a gradient of black, fading on the more distant area, where a hint of powder blue establishes the finished look of the shaded area.

Fig. 3-47. Remove frisket from the sunlit side.

Fig. 3-42.

Fig. 3-43.

Fig. 3-44.

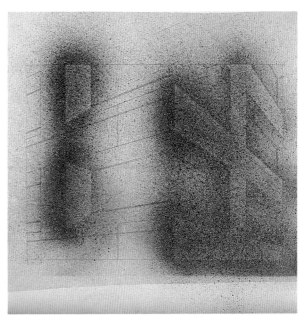

Fig. 3-46.

Fig. 3-45.

Fig. 3-47.

Fig. 3-48.

Fig. 3-49.

Fig. 3-50.

Fig. 3-48. Load the airbrush with flesh color and apply an even coat.

Fig. 3-49. Protect the exposed finished side with pieces of cardboard and splatter a coarse but light coat of brown over the flesh base tone. This supplies the harsh contrasting shadows cast by the aggregate.

Fig. 3-50. Remove all frisket.

Fig. 3-51. Refrisket the entire piece, cut outlines to complete the remaining precast surfaces, and expose the areas in cast shadow. Apply brown to the areas of cast shadow.

Fig. 3-52. Add a splatter of flesh color to soften the area.

Fig. 3-53. Spray a coarse coating of black; this cast shadow area will become the darkest part of the finished illustration.

Fig. 3-54. Remove the frisket from the soffit and apply a coat of brown.

Fig. 3-51.

Fig. 3-53.

Fig. 3-52.

Fig. 3-54.

Fig. 3-55. Add a light coat of flesh tone to the soffit area.

Fig. 3-56. Apply a delicate coat of black to retain the quality of reflected light in the upper right. The soffit will be lighter than the cast shadow.

Fig. 3-57. Remove the film from the shaded portion of the last remaining precast piece, the sloping surface. This is the lightest part of the illustration.

Fig. 3-58. Add a spatter of brown to the shaded side.

Fig. 3-59. Follow with a much lighter application of brown on the sunlit side. Next, spray the sunlit side with a fine coating of flesh tone. Apply the sliver of cast shadow with the aid of a piece of cardboard.

Fig. 3-60. Remove the frisket.

Fig. 3-55.

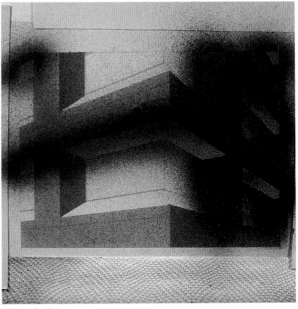

Fig. 3-56.

Fig. 3-57.

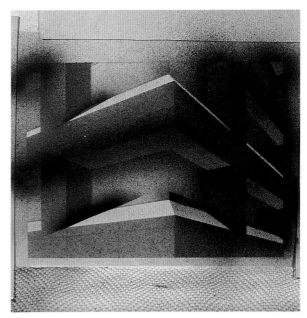

Fig. 3-59.

Fig. 3-58.

Fig. 3-60.

Fig. 3-61. Apply new frisket and expose the glazing in shade.

Fig. 3-62. Adjust the air pressure to about 35 psi. Apply a smooth graded tone of powder blue, followed by a spray of black, with the aid of a precut piece of cardboard, to establish the wavy outlines of reflections. Spray a hint of brown in the corners to pick up on the color of the precast. Add a fine graded tone of black at the lower left of the glazing as the finishing touch.

Fig. 3-63. Uncover the remaining glazing, then spray on a light coat of flesh tone. Protect the dark side of the illustration with a piece of cardboard.

Fig. 3-64. Using the same piece of cardboard, apply the cast shadows and reflections with black.

Fig. 3-65. Spray in powder blue to add a hint of sky. Lower the black horizontal shadow line to coincide with the reflection on the glazing in shade.

Fig. 3-66. Remove the frisket.

Fig. 3-61.

Fig. 3-62.

Fig. 3-63.

Fig. 3-65.

Fig. 3-64.

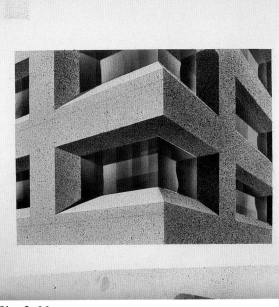

Fig. 3-66.

Fig. 3-67. With a ruling pen and a combination of brown and black, draw the mullions. Using a mixture of black, brown, and flesh, add the precast joints. Use a mix of white and flesh tone to highlight the edges of the joints.

Fig. 3-68. Apply a coat of acrylic varnish. The example is now finished.

Fig. 3-67.

Fig. 3-68.

Exercise 2: A Glass Facade

As the previous exercise just demonstrated, glass is a complex surface to render well. Not only is it transparent, it also reflects. Its reflections, however, are usually distorted, a straight line becoming wavy. My best advice is to be observant. There is glass all around you—in cities, shopping centers, business districts, residential neighborhoods. Study it in all lights and environments. In this exercise, you will work on a corner of a glass building. The reflections on the surface allude to structures across the street and to portions of this building, which are mirrored in the sunlit part of the glass.

Palette: Winsor & Newton acrylic sap green; Badger Air-Opaque aqua, black, white, blue, flesh, and powder blue.

Fig. 3-69. Cut and remove the frisket from the sunlit part. Use a mixture of aqua, sap green, and black to lay in the reflections, with the aid of a precut piece of cardboard.

Fig. 3-70. Add the beginnings of distant reflections. With the help of the same piece of cardboard, apply a light spray of powder blue. The glass is now beginning to look realistic.

Fig. 3-69.

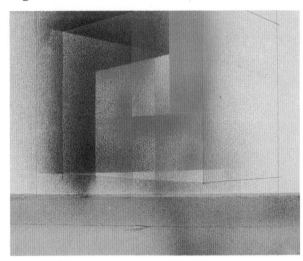

Fig. 3-70.

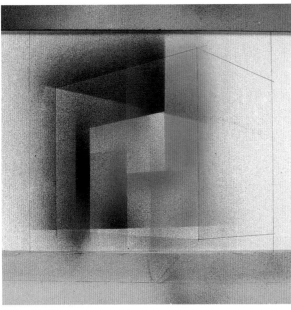

Fig. 3-71.

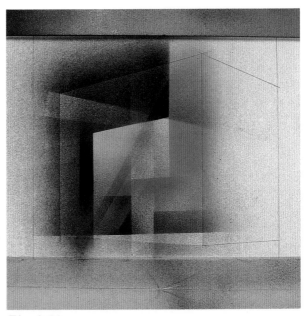

Fig. 3-72.

Fig. 3-71. Strengthen some of the shades
with a mixture of black, aqua, and blue.

Fig. 3-72. With the same mixture, add some
horizontal reflections and a diagonal reflection, suggesting secondary light reflection
from across the street.

Fig. 3-73. Using prepared cardboard and a
mix of powder blue and white, add wavy
reflections for the sidewalk and pavement.
Add more dark reflections to the light area
near the corner, and add a diagonal stripe to
strengthen the reflections from across the
street.

Fig. 3-73.

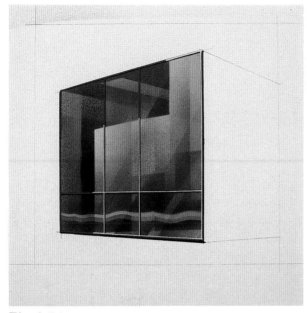

Fig. 3-74.

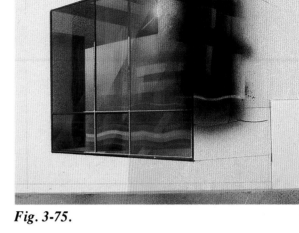

Fig. 3-75.

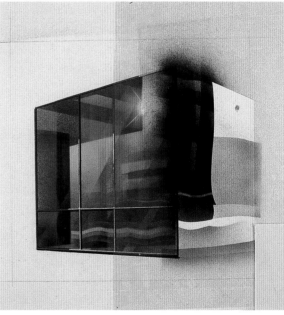

Fig. 3-74. After the frisket is removed, it becomes apparent that more work needs to be done. Add mullions with a mixture of flesh, white, and black. With the original mixture of black, aqua, and blue, add some horizontal stripes. Add a spray of pure white for the sunburst peeking around the corner.

Fig. 3-75. Cut the frisket on the shaded side to suggest wavy images. Create reflections in the shaded side with black. Spray over the black with a mixture of aqua, green, and black.

Fig. 3-76. Remove the rest of the frisket from the right side. Add reflections with a light mixture of aqua, green, and black. Use precut pieces of cardboard.

Fig. 3-76.

Fig. 3-77. Add and define more reflections with the dark mix. Follow this by adding highlights, horizontal and diagonal stripes with light applications of powder blue and white.

Fig. 3-78. Add the mullions with a ruling pen. Use pure black, powder blue, and white to create highlights on the leading edges.

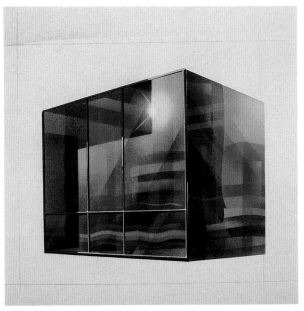

Fig. 3-77.

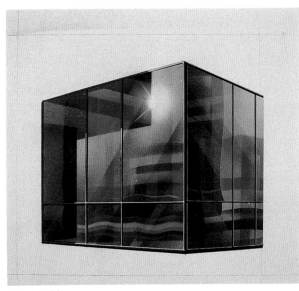

Fig. 3-78.

Exercise 3: An Afternoon Sky

Landscapes and sky-scapes are an integral part of architectural illustration. They make the building come to life. Rendering the sky also offers a pleasant reward—a place where you can let your creativity have free reign, as long as the results do not overwhelm the architectural subject. An afternoon sky is one of my favorites. On sunny days, it is often studded with fair-weather clouds, and it produces the shadows that often bring out the best in a building. In this exercise, the project was an aerial view of a design for the Honda Corporation headquarters near Torrance, California. I worked on the sky area first, and that's all that need concern you here. I have included, however, step-by-step instructions of the land and buildings in case you would like to try your hand at rendering these as well.

Palette (acrylic colors): payne's gray, cerulean blue, phthalocyanine blue, alizarin crimson, naples yellow, burnt umber, and white.

Fig. 3-79. The layout is copied onto the support.

Fig. 3-80. A piece of scrap mat board with a straight edge supplies the horizon line. Adjust the air pressure on your airbrush to the lowest psi to achieve a smooth spray. Use a mixture of phthalocyanine blue, cerulean blue, and white for the background. Lighten the horizon with white and a touch of naples yellow.

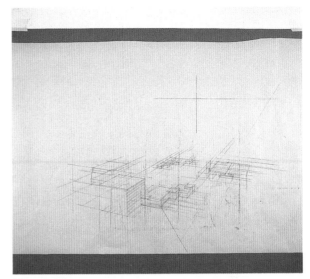

Fig. 3-79.

Fig. 3-80.

Fig. 3-81. Spray in the beginnings of cumulus clouds with the same mixture of white and naples yellow.

Fig. 3-82. The buildup of clouds is akin to the happy accident in fine art. You have to let your instincts take over; build up the clouds little by little until they look right. The highlights are white with a minute quantity of naples yellow. Here is where the reduced air pressure helps alleviate the problem of spreading accumulated paint. Hold the airbrush close to the surface, very much like in the dot and line exercises.

Fig. 3-83. The cloud bases and shadows are added with payne's gray, cerulean blue, white, and alizarin crimson. This adds three-dimensionality to the sky. The technique is the same as for the highlights.

Fig. 3-84. The distant ocean is sprayed in a diffuse application of phthalocyanine blue, cerulean blue, and white. The rest of the illustration is painted with filament brushes, save for some cast shadows on the roof surfaces and the textures of the parking lots and roads. The background is painted in watercolor style with a Chinese watercolor brush of immense proportion (roughly the equivalent of our #24).

Fig. 3-85. Background details are added very quickly with smaller filament brushes, the landscape with #10 and #12 round sable brushes, and the suggestions of buildings with #10 and ½″ to ¾″ flats. The roofs are frisketed, cut, and painted with a 1″ flat brush, working very quickly to achieve the striations and tonal differences.

Fig. 3-86. After the roofs dry, frisket and airbrush the shadows with a mixture of payne's gray and burnt umber.

Fig. 3-81.

Fig. 3-82.

Fig. 3-83.

Fig. 3-85.

Fig. 3-84.

Fig. 3-86.

Fig. 3-87.

Fig. 3-87. The finished illustration.

4

DEMONSTRATIONS FROM THE PROJECT FILE

With few exceptions, the exercises in previous chapters have all focused on imaginary buildings and surfaces. While these can be instructive in the manipulation of tools and media, there is no substitute for the real thing. In this chapter, I have culled six assignments from my own project file, arranged in order of increasing complexity. For each one, I will give you a list of the materials and tools I used and will take you step by step through the completion of the assignment. The insight gained will help you create your own assignments and get improved results.

Project 1: School Addition

Client: McClellan Cruz Gaylord Associates,
    Architects
Location: Pasadena, California
Airbrush: Paasche Model H with #1 spray tip
Ground: Crescent No. 110 illustration board
Palette: Tube acrylics, diluted—burnt siena,
    burnt umber, cadmium orange, cadmium
    yellow light, payne's gray
Frisket: Graphix prepared frisket
Dimensions of artwork: 22 by 32 inches

Overview: This project is a perfect example
of the airbrush's compatibility with illustration
—an otherwise ordinary sketch became something unexpected. An addition was to be made
to an existing building. The illustration was to
be done in two stages: first, a finished ink
drawing was to be made for black-and-white
reproduction; second, a full-color illustration
was to be added to the drawing. The most
suitable medium for this type of assignment is
transparent paint. Thanks to the airbrush, the
coloring took less than three hours and is
really quite simple to produce. The only tricky
passages are where surfaces are curved.

Fig. 4-1. The completed ink drawing. Note
the careful rendering and shading of details.
Using transparent colors allows you to benefit
from this painstaking work. The surface
details will be visible through the paint layers.

Fig. 4-2. The addition was to be brick and I
had been given a brick sample as a color
guide. I was able to match this color with
coats of four colors (clockwise from lower
left): color 1, a mix of cadmium yellow light,
cadmium orange, and burnt siena for the highlights; color 2, burnt siena for the base color;
color 3, a mix of burnt siena, burnt umber,
and payne's gray for open shade; and color 4,
a mix of burnt umber and payne's gray for
cast shadows.

Fig. 4-1.

Fig. 4-2.

Fig. 4-3. The entire drawing has been covered with a sheet of preglued frisket. This was then cut and removed from the areas of open shade (with the exception of the area to the left of the doorway, which will be dealt with in the next step), and a coat of color 3 has been applied. I then airbrushed in the cast shadows with color 4.

Fig. 4-4. . . . and airbrushed the area of light shade to the left of the doorway, using color 3. Note that this is a curved building unit, essentially a cylinder. If you have any doubts about how to produce this effect, go back and review the cylinder exercise in chapter 2.

Fig. 4-3.

Fig. 4-4.

Fig. 4-5.

Fig. 4-6.

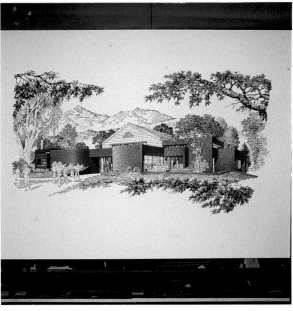

Fig. 4-7.

Fig. 4-5. Without frisketing the work just completed, I airbrushed in the sunlit areas with color 1. Using this base color, I finished the surfaces in the background first, applying lighter and lighter coats as I worked on the surfaces in the foreground, closest to the viewer.

Fig. 4-6. The curved surface to the right of the doorway where the sun hits the curvature is the lightest.

Fig. 4-7. All the friskets have been removed but the drawing is not quite finished.

Fig. 4-8.

Fig. 4-8. The finishing touches were made with a sable watercolor brush, adding just a hint of color to the people's clothing and the windows, and giving light washes of color to the landscape.

Project 2: Medical Building

Client: Medical Planning Associates
Location: Denver, Colorado
Airbrush: Paasche Model H
Ground: Crescent colored mat board
Palette: cerulean blue, phthalocyanine blue,
   alizarin crimson, naples yellow, white,
   burnt umber, payne's gray, cadmium yellow
   light
Frisket: preglued film, scraps of torn blotter
Dimensions of artwork: 24 by 36 inches

Overview: This building is located in the
environs of Denver. I have used artistic
license to bring the Rocky Mountains in the
background a bit closer than they are in real-
ity. I chose a warm-colored mat board to
counteract the chilly feeling of the snow-cov-
ered peaks.

Fig. 4-9. Using a carbon transfer, I copied
the building layout onto the mat board. The
building was then covered with frisket and a
base coat of sky color (cerulean blue, phthalocyanine blue, alizarin crimson, and white) was
airbrushed on.

Fig. 4-10. Cloud shadows were airbrushed
in with a mixture of cerulean blue, phthalocyanine blue, and alizarin crimson.

Fig. 4-11. Using a piece of torn blotting
paper, I begin to establish the outlines and
forms of the clouds.

Fig. 4-12. The outlines of the Rockies are
also produced with pieces of torn blotting
paper. I like to use more than one blotter-
paper frisket to ensure a realistic variety of
outlines, whether in sky or mountain.

Fig. 4-13. Highlights are added to the
clouds in successive layers of naples yellow
and white. This is a time-consuming part of
the project; applying too much highlight tone
in a single layer may result in puddling, an
effect you want to avoid.

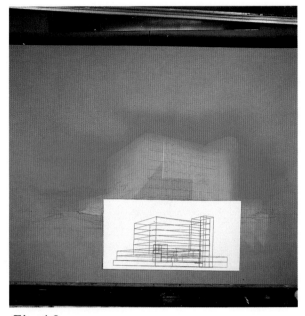

Fig. 4-9.

Fig. 4-10.

Fig. 4-12.

Fig. 4-11.

Fig. 4-13.

Fig. 4-14. I have painted in the grass and trees using a regular sable watercolor brush with chrome oxide green, sap green, burnt umber, yellow ochre, burnt siena, red oxide, cadmium yellow medium, and payne's gray. These areas have been covered with frisket to protect them. The street is stippled with the airbrush in payne's gray and burnt umber.

Fig. 4-15. The sidewalk is defined, using strips of leftover mat board and white, cerulean blue, payne's gray, and burnt umber.

Fig. 4-16. When I removed the frisket from the building, I discovered a splotch of paint. This sometimes happens. I just work right over it and it will never be noticed in the final illustration.

Fig. 4-17. The far sidewalk, rocks, and minor details of the surroundings are painted in.

Fig. 4-18. The precast is started with naples yellow and payne's gray.

Fig. 4-19. The upper right part of the building is getting a heavy coat of pure white.

Fig. 4-14.

Fig. 4-15.

Fig. 4-16.

Fig. 4-18.

Fig. 4-17.

Fig. 4-19.

Fig. 4-20. The shadows on the sunscreen were penciled in before airbrushing with burnt umber and payne's gray. A piece of cardboard with a shadow-shaped window cut out makes a practical frisket for this step.

Fig. 4-21. The sunlit precast section with all shadows added. The elevator core will be added in a separate step, since it is a cylindrical form and would be difficult to work on with the adjacent finished precast exposed.

Fig. 4-22. The side of the building in open shade is worked on just as the sun-facing side was, using payne's gray, cerulean blue, white, and burnt umber.

Fig. 4-23. The frisket is removed, exposing the elevator core, windows, and canopy.

Fig. 4-24. The elevator core is finished as a cylinder, using payne's gray, burnt umber, cerulean blue, and white in shade that is gradually lightened with repeated vertical passages of naples yellow and white.

Fig. 4-25. The windows are finished in one frisketing step. The base color is payne's gray and burnt umber; cool reflections are added with cerulean blue, phthalocyanine blue, and white. Warm diffuse interior light on shaded areas is achieved by spraying over the shade with a mix of cadmium yellow medium, burnt umber, and white. The sunlit highlights are cadmium yellow medium and white. The entrance canopy, the last portion of the building to be finished, was done with white, naples yellow, burnt umber, and cerulean blue.

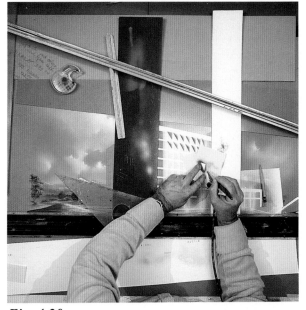

Fig. 4-20.

Fig. 4-21.

Fig. 4-22.

Fig. 4-24.

Fig. 4-23.

Fig. 4-25.

Fig. 4-26.

Fig. 4-26. The finished illustration. I have
painted in a few cars and people and given a
touch of redwood to the sidewalk area. For
this I used a sable watercolor brush and pure
colors from the palette used for the rest of this
exercise.

Project 3: Airport Hotel

Client: Herbert Nadel, A.I.A. & Partners
Location: Los Angeles, California
Airbrush: Paasche Model H
Ground: Strathmore cold-pressed illustration
    board
Palette: Alizarin crimson, black, burnt umber,
    cadmium yellow light, cerulean blue, cobalt
    blue, naples yellow, payne's gray, phthalo-
    cyanine blue, phthalocyanine green, powder
    blue (Badger Air-Opaque), unbleached tita-
    nium, white, and yellow ochre
Frisket: Graphix prepared frisket
Dimensions of artwork: 23 by 40 inches

Overview: This project is good practice in
producing a many-windowed facade. I was
also instructed to make a new building appear
mellowed with age, a look the architects envi-
sioned for the finished building.

Fig. 4-27. Because I did not have any color
samples, I rendered a corner detail of the
building to serve as color reference. This was
photographed and sent to the client for
approval and comment. This little tip can save
an illustrator a lot of extra work redoing a
project later.

Fig. 4-28. I first prepared a detailed ink
drawing.

Fig. 4-27.

Fig. 4-28.

Fig. 4-29. From the skyline down, I covered the main drawing with a frisket to allow myself to airbrush the sky first, applying a graduated tone of the base color: a mix of white, cerulean, phthalocyanine blue, and powder blue. This was applied in several layers, darker at the top, fading out toward the horizon. The piece of scrap board was used as a test area.

Fig. 4-30. I painted in the dark foreground tree with a sable watercolor brush, using payne's gray, alizarin crimson, and burnt umber. The light foreground tree was painted with chrome oxide green, burnt umber, and yellow ochre. To save time, the ink drawing was done last, right over the paint, which in turn had been applied right over the sky. At this stage, I also worked on the clouds, using white, burnt umber, payne's gray, powder blue, crimson, and naples yellow.

Fig. 4-31. The frisket is removed from the roof areas of the building.

Fig. 4-32. A coat of payne's gray, cobalt blue, phthalocyanine green, and alizarin crimson is applied to the areas of open shade on the roof. This color mix gave me the bluish hue the client had approved. I used a piece of cardboard to protect the unfrisketed areas.

Fig. 4-33. The sunlit sides of the roof are given a lighter coat of the same color mix. Cast shadows are added with cobalt blue, payne's gray, phthalocyanine green, and white. A cardboard frisket, cut to shape, keeps the lines sharp. The standing seams in the roof are added with a ruling pen.

Fig. 4-29.

Fig. 4-30.

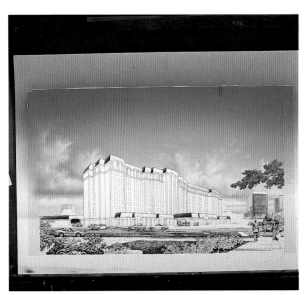

Fig. 4-32.

Fig. 4-31.

Fig. 4-33.

Fig. 4-34. The frisket was removed from the building, which was given a base coat of stucco color—a mix of white, unbleached titanium, naples yellow, and a touch of alizarin crimson. I refrisketed the roof using scraps of board and paper. Using a plastic triangle to keep the edges crisp, I established the areas of open shade with a coat of payne's gray, burnt umber, and black. To get a stucco effect, I lowered the air pressure and opened the airbrush tip slightly.

Fig. 4-35. For a change of pace, I switched to the peripheral areas in the drawing, adding touches of yellow ochre, chrome oxide green, payne's gray, phthalocyanine blue, and alizarin crimson to the landscape, people, cars, and background buildings. The parking garage (left) had been left unpainted to this point while the client decided on color. That decision having now been made, I filled in the structure with the same colors as the main building.

Fig. 4-34.

Fig. 4-35.

Fig. 4-36. Back to work on the building facade, I have added the cast shadows to the sunlit side, using payne's gray, burnt umber, and black. Because of the configuration of the cornice, the edges of these shadows are not straight. I had to frisket the area again before airbrushing.

Fig. 4-37. There's no putting it off any longer—the windows must be worked on. I covered the building with a new frisket and painstakingly cut openings for each window, counting myself lucky to need only one frisketing for this project. (In other projects, the windows have required several frisketings, one for each step.) I applied color here in a sequence of layers: dark tones and cast shadows in payne's gray and burnt umber; highlights in pthalocyanine blue, powder blue, and white; reflections in white, naples yellow, and alizarin crimson; and the sunburst in white. The sunburst was rendered with a fine spray in concentric applications. I held the airbrush 2 inches back from the center and 6 inches back from the fringes, to reduce color saturation.

Fig. 4-36.

Fig. 4-37.

Fig. 4-38.

Fig. 4-38. The finished drawing. In the final
step, I added the construction joints, the
reveals, and the cast shadows around the windows, using a ruling pen for these details. I
also filled in the missing bits and pieces, such
as the landscape that overlaps the building.

Project 4: Glass and Concrete Office Building

Client: John Siebel A.I.A.
Location: Tarzana, California
Airbrush: Paasche Model H, #1 spray tip
Ground: Crescent No. 110 illustration board
Palette: Alizarin crimson, cerulean blue, dioxazine purple, payne's gray, phthalocyanine blue, burnt umber, cadmium yellow light, and white
Frisket: Preglued sheets of film
Other tools and supplies: Filament brushes, ruling pen
Dimensions of artwork: 22 by 34 inches

Overview: In this project, I will concentrate on illustrating glass with the combined use of airbrush and filament brushes, for the reflections and tonal qualities would be too difficult and time-consuming to render well with the sole use of either tool.

Fig. 4-39. The building was frisketed, then the sky was established, using only the airbrush and following the same steps as in previous projects. The sky colors are a mix of cerulean blue, phthalocyanine blue, alizarin crimson, and white; the clouds are a combination of payne's gray, alizarin crimson, burnt umber, dioxazine purple, white, and naples yellow. Next, I used an assortment of filament brushes to paint in the street and the trees behind the building.

Fig. 4-40. The airbrush was also used to stipple the street with a mixture of alizarin crimson, payne's gray, and burnt umber.

Fig. 4-39.

Fig. 4-40.

Fig. 4-41. The used frisket is removed from the building and a fresh sheet applied.

Fig. 4-42. The outline of the glass areas is cut and the frisket removed from them. I then used a wide flat watercolor brush to apply a mix of payne's gray, alizarin crimson, cerulean blue, and phthalocyanine blue in quick vertical strokes.

Fig. 4-43. The frisket is removed and again new frisket is applied to the building facade.

Fig. 4-44. The shadows cast on the glazing by the overhangs and columns are cut, exposed, and airbrushed with payne's gray and burnt umber.

Fig. 4-45. The remaining frisket is removed from the glass areas.

Fig. 4-46. Using an assortment of brushes, I painted in details, particularly on the street level where there is much reflection. My decisions are based on many hours spent observing the patterns of reflection on glass surfaces. I also photograph windows in various lights and study the reflections as they appear in the photographs.

Fig. 4-41.

Fig. 4-42.

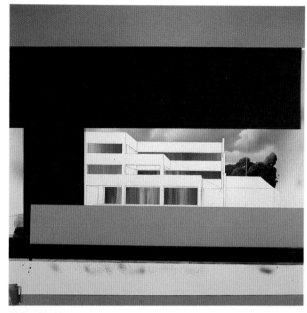

Fig. 4-43.

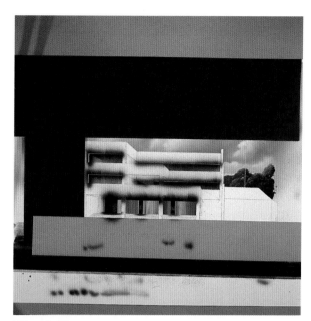

Fig. 4-45.

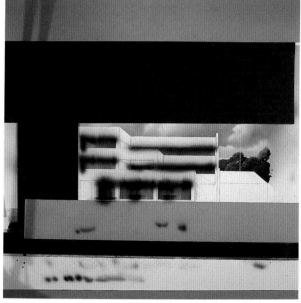

Fig. 4-44.

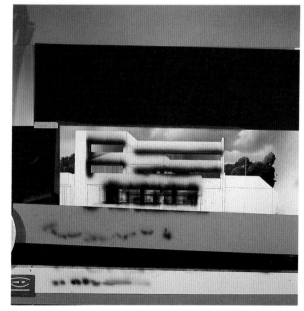

Fig. 4-46.

Fig. 4-47. More detail is added to the window areas.

Fig. 4-48. The glass is finished and the frisket removed.

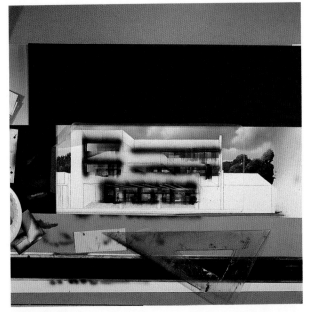

Fig. 4-47.

Fig. 4-48.

Fig. 4-49.

Fig. 4-49. The final drawing. I have used the airbrush to stipple on open shade and cast shadows and have put on the finishing touches with various tools. For the construction joints and first-floor mullions, I used a ruling pen; for the adjoining buildings, plants, cars, and people, I used watercolor brushes.

Project 5: Brick Office Building

Client: Herbert Nadel A.I.A. & Partners
Location: Sherman Oaks, California
Airbrush: Paasche Model H
Ground: Crescent No. 110 illustration board
Palette (acrylic colors): Cerulean blue, cobalt
    blue, ultramarine blue, phthalocyanine blue,
    alizarin crimson, white, naples yellow,
    payne's gray, burnt umber, black, scarlet,
    burnt siena, raw siena, cadmium yellow
    medium, chrome oxide green, and sap green
Frisket: Graphix prepared frisket
Dimensions of artwork: 24 by 36 inches

Fig. 4-50.

Overview: As in project 4, a combination of
airbrush and regular brushes was needed to
complete this project. In this case, the airbrush was more of an auxiliary tool, but it
saved a great deal of time in working on the
sky, adding texture to the facade, and creating
reflections on the glass. My plan was to complete the entire environment of this building—
background landscape, foreground street, and
sky—before working on the building itself.

Fig. 4-50. I transferred the building layout
to the illustration board with carbon transfer,
using a blueline print of the original layout
approved by the client. I covered the building
with frisket, cutting the outline and removing
the fringes. I painted in the street with a large
Chinese watercolor brush, using black, burnt
umber, raw siena, scarlet, cobalt blue, phthalocyanine blue, and white. The shadows on the
middle right were added with large, flat watercolor brushes.

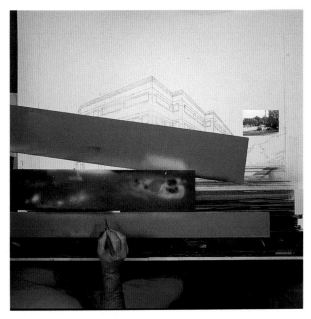

Fig. 4-51.

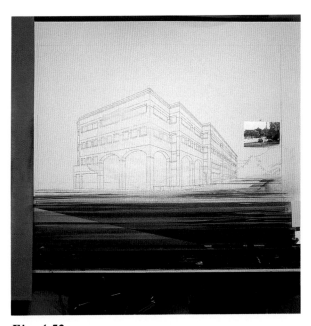

Fig. 4-52.

Fig. 4-51. Using long scraps of straight-edged mat boards, I airbrushed in the sidewalk, along with the street textures. I sprayed the highlights on the sidewalk with a mixture of cobalt blue, phthalocyanine blue, and white. The colors shown here are diluted mixtures of the colors listed in figure 4-50.

Fig. 4-52. The result of the sequence described in the previous two captions.

Fig. 4-53. Some adjustments are made to the elongated shadows on the sidewalk, using mixes of the blues, reds, and black listed in the palette.

Fig. 4-53.

Fig. 4-54. I have finished the sidewalk and am making progress on the street.

Fig. 4-55. Some of the elongated shadows on the street are truncated, their edges sharpened with the same dark mix as before. A dark stipple is added to suggest pavement texture.

Fig. 4-56. The finished streetscape.

Fig. 4-57. The sky was airbrushed in, using the same colors and technique as in earlier projects. (See, for example, project 1.) The background landscape was painted in with brushes, and the frisket was then removed from the building.

Fig. 4-58. I applied a new frisket and cut out the areas in open shade. With a 1-inch flat brush, I applied the brick color—a mixture of burnt siena, burnt umber, payne's gray, scarlet, and a touch of white. A mixture of diluted burnt umber, burnt siena, and white is applied with the airbrush to give aggregate to the brick. The airbrush nozzle is given a three-quarters turn, and the spray is applied very lightly at about 15 psi air pressure. I then rule in the brick lines.

Fig. 4-54.

Fig. 4-55.

Fig. 4-57.

Fig. 4-56.

Fig. 4-58.

Fig. 4-59. The frisket is now removed from the sunlit side and a new sheet of frisket is applied. The sunlit brick is exposed and with the wide, flat filament brush, a graduated tone is painted in on quick diagonal strokes, light shades at the upper right gradually becoming darker toward the lower left. The colors are the same as on the shaded side, but the mix is much brighter here—I add an increased concentration of burnt siena, cadmium yellow medium, scarlet, raw siena, and white. It is important to experiment with colors, as brush-applied colors have a certain "happy accident" quality. Using brushes, you can reproduce two panels that are similar in appearance but not identical.

Fig. 4-60. I apply a light stipple, using raw siena, cadmium yellow medium, and white to add highlights and the appearance of aggregate, making sure that I have opened the airbrush nozzle three-quarters of the way and set the air pressure at 15 psi. I rule in the brick lines with a ruling pen and a mixture of naples yellow, white, burnt umber, and payne's gray.

Fig. 4-59.

Fig. 4-60.

Fig. 4-61. The upper-floor fenestration and the simple first-floor glazing are added with one frisketing and a mix of black, payne's gray, and cerulean blue. The highlight of the upper middle part of the sunlit side is a mixture of naples yellow and white. I increased the air pressure to 25 psi for this and adjusted the airbrush nozzle back a half-turn, to ensure a smooth spray.

Fig. 4-62. The indoor activity is painted onto the arched fenestration with filament brushes. Highlights are airbrushed in with varying mixtures of blues, black, naples yellow, and white. Notice how in airbrushing with a few pieces of cardboard, the upper, more reflective, parts of the glass are clearly separated from the see-through portions. The cast shadow is shown on the top-floor windows; the line of glass on the floor below is shown without shadow.

Fig. 4-61.

Fig. 4-62.

Fig. 4-63.

Fig. 4-63. The completed building. The trees, plants, cars, and people were painted with filament brushes to add scale and activity. I made a careful inspection of the illustration and marked mistakes and blemishes on a see-through acetate overlay for reference and later correction. With a complex building like this, some mistakes will be overlooked no matter how carefully you examine the illustration. After you have worked on a project for a few days, your eye gets used to the appearance of the project and it is easy to overlook errors. Try to schedule your time so that you finish complicated projects a few days before the deadline. Set the illustration aside for a day or two, then check for more mistakes. You'll be surprised by the number of blemishes and mistakes that become obvious after you have taken a short break from the project.

Project 6: A Downtown Plaza

Client: Langdon Wilson Mumper Architects
Location: Glendale, California
Airbrush: Paasche Model H
Ground: Strathmore illustration board
Palette: Black, burnt siena, burnt umber, cerulean blue, dioxazine purple, naples yellow, payne's gray, phthalocyanine blue, raw siena, scarlet, unbleached titanium, vermilion, and white
Dimensions of artwork: 27 by 38 inches

Overview: This project is a lesson in rendering complicated areas of brickwork. The view is a public square between twin office towers with a connecting glass structure. The primary building material for both pavement and towers is brick. The project required quite a bit of preliminary work. An ink drawing of the project was prepared and used in black-and-white form as a cover sheet on the construction documents. The brick pavement was drawn in ink. This meant that transparent colors had to be used to allow the ink lines to show through.

Fig. 4-64. I decided that long shadows and the soft light of sunset would best suit this scene. The sky was therefore airbrushed with a mix of dioxazine purple, cerulean blue, and phthalocyanine blue at the top, gradually changing to a mix of naples yellow, scarlet, and white to get the setting-sun effect. Here I am working on the darkest areas of the buildings. The inkwork is visible as I begin coloring the shaded side of the brick. The brick sample supplied by the client was matched with mixtures of burnt siena, burnt umber, vermilion, and raw siena. Payne's gray and burnt umber were used for shadows. The brick color was sprayed first, followed by the shade color.

Fig. 4-65. I use a piece of cardboard to obtain a sharp separation between the soffit and adjoining surface as I apply the shade color.

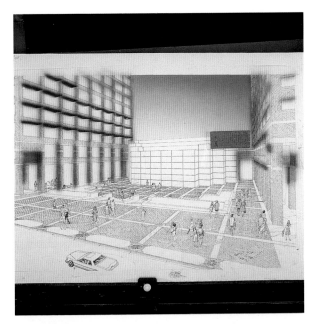

Fig. 4-64.

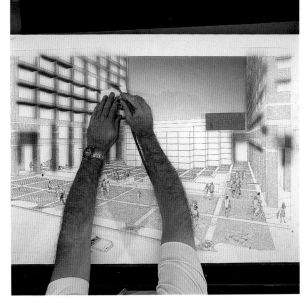

Fig. 4-65.

Fig. 4-66. I darken the vertical brick reveal since it is in cast shadow and will appear darker than the face of the building. (See figure 4-72 for the finished effect.)

Fig. 4-67. I complete the diagonal cast shadows by adding shade colors, having sprayed the red brick color earlier.

Fig. 4-68. The frisket is removed from the cast shadows on the ground plane. Here, the order of color application is reversed in order to complete the pavement in one frisketing. The shadow color is applied and the remaining frisket is removed from the brickwork only.

Figs. 4-69 and 4-70. I apply the "paver" color—the basic brick color darkened somewhat with burnt umber and payne's gray. I set the air pressure on the airbrush at about 15 psi and use a fairly coarse spray to show some granular effect.

Fig. 4-71. The street is uncovered. I apply the same shade used for the brick in a dark-to-light pattern, opening the airbrush nozzle slightly to obtain a coarser spray to simulate the pavement.

Fig. 4-66.

Fig. 4-67.

Fig. 4-68.

Fig. 4-70.

Fig. 4-69.

Fig. 4-71.

Fig. 4-72.

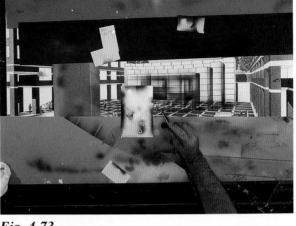

Fig. 4-73.

Fig. 4-74.

Fig. 4-72. Before the frisket is removed, the background trees are added. Now the entire illustration is uncovered, debris removed. I airbrush the people in bright colors from the palette. This is a bit of relief from the monotony of the brickwork.

Fig. 4-73. A new sheet of frisket is applied and the work begins on the central glass atrium. This is a rather complicated combination of overlapping and receding planes, requiring several frisketings to obtain a clean separation and definition of the elements. The cast shadows and front facade get a dark spray of payne's gray and burnt umber. I block in major reflections, including the pavers visible in the glass, with the leftover colors mixed for the outside pavers.

Fig. 4-74. Transparent sunset colors are sprayed over the glass.

Fig. 4-75.

Fig. 4-76.

Fig. 4-77.

Fig. 4-75. With cardboard blocks, some interior details are painted in, using light opaque mixes of white, cerulean blue, and naples yellow.

Fig. 4-76. I spray tested the airbrush for the next color, the amber reflections on the shaded side of the glass and on the inside surface visible through the facade on the left. The mirror in this figure is used to check the work on reverse; this tends to make problems developing in the illustration more apparent to the illustrator.

Fig. 4-77. A mix of payne's gray and burnt umber has been applied to the inside face, and sunset colors sprayed on the right side panels. The remaining glass panels of the atrium are finished in a like manner.

Fig. 4-78.

Fig. 4-79.

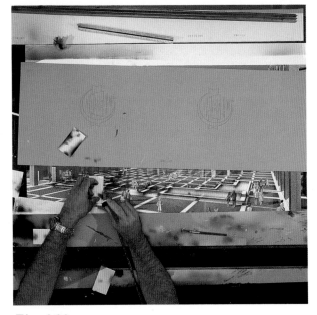

Fig. 4-80.

Fig. 4-78. The fenestration is completed on the left side facade, using the same color mixes utilized on the atrium. The translucence is achieved with a dark spray of payne's gray and burnt umber, illustrating the return of the facade on the far side, visible through the glass. The reflections of the tower on the right are added, the shadows and the sunlit portions of the glass are finished on the right side, and the frisket is removed.

Fig. 4-79. The fountain details are finished with greens from the palette, using techniques very much like those in the marble exercises. However, instead of veining, an aggregate is sprayed, with later coats of opaque highlights used to simulate the polished quality of the material.

Fig. 4-80. The top surface of the granite is finished with the same techniques as in the preceding areas.

Fig. 4-81.

Fig. 4-81. The water is painted in with filament brushes, using white, phthalocyanine green, cerulean blue, payne's gray, and a touch of naples yellow for a glint of sunlight. Trees are added on the plaza to complete the pictures, using greens and yellows from the palette for the warm-colored trees in sunlight. Cool greens, tempered with the palette blues and payne's gray, are used for the trees in shade.

5

A PORTFOLIO OF ARCHITECTURAL ILLUSTRATION

Fig. 5-1. Filipinas Plaza
Location: Los Angeles, California
Client: Langdon Wilson Mumper Architects
Airbrush: Paasche Model H used on sky, pre-
    cast, and glazing
Ground: Crescent No. 110 illustration board
Media: Tube and liquid acrylics applied with
    airbrush and filament brushes

Fig. 5-2. Santa Monica Medical Building
Location: Santa Monica, California
Client: Langdon Wilson Mumper Architects
Airbrush: Paasche Model H used on sky, pre-
   cast, and glazing
Ground: Strathmore cold-pressed illustration
   board
Media: Tube and liquid acrylics applied with
   airbrush and filament brushes

Fig. 5-3. Sierra Medical Center
Location: El Paso, Texas
Client: Langdon Wilson Mumper Architects
Airbrush: Paasche Model H used on sky,
    stucco, and fenestration
Ground: Crescent No. 110 illustration board
Media: Tube and liquid acrylics applied with
    airbrush and filament brushes

Fig. 5-4. Condominium Project
Location: Virginia Beach, Virginia
Client: Jose Francisco Soria, A.I.A.
Airbrush: Paasche Model H used on sky and
    stucco
Ground: Crescent No. 110 illustration board
Medium: Tube acrylics applied with airbrush
    and filament brushes

Fig. 5-5. Finch Hall, Fuller Theological
    Seminary
Location: Pasadena, California
Client: Kurt Meyer F.I.A.A. & Partners
Airbrush: Paasche Model VL used on sky,
    stucco, glazing, sidewalk, and pavement
Ground: Strathmore cold-pressed illustration
    board
Media: Liquid acrylics applied with airbrush
    on building and sky; tube acrylics applied
    with filament brushes on entourage

Fig. 5-6. 1145 Wilshire Boulevard
Location: Los Angeles, California
Client: Langdon Wilson Mumper Architects
Airbrush: Paasche Model H used on sky, granite, glazing, and high-rise building in background
Ground: Strathmore cold-pressed illustration board
Media: Liquid and tube acrylics applied with airbrush on buildings and sky; tube acrylics applied with filament brushes on rest of entourage

Fig. 5-7. Los Robles Office Building
Location: Pasadena, California
Client: Langdon Wilson Mumper Architects
Airbrush: Paasche Model H used on sky,
    granite, and glazing
Ground: Crescent No. 110 illustration board
Media: Tube and liquid acrylics used on sky
    and building; tube acrylics applied with fila-
    ment brushes on entourage.

Fig. 5-8. Glendale Square Lobby
Location: Glendale, California
Client: Langdon Wilson Mumper Architects
Airbrush: Paasche Models H and VL used on
  sky, brick, concrete, pavement, and glazing
Ground: Strathmore cold-pressed illustration
  board
Liquid frisket: Grumbacher Miskit applied to
  separate trees and people from background
Media: Liquid and tube acrylics

Fig. 5-9. Conrad International and Jupiter's Casino
Location: Gold Coast, Brisbane, Australia
Client: Hilton Hotel Corporation
Airbrush: Thayer & Chandler Model A used on building; Paasche Model H used on sky

Ground: Strathmore cold-pressed illustration board
Liquid frisket: Grumbacher Miskit used to separate trees from background
Medium: Tube acrylics

Fig. 5-10. Hilton Hotel and Casino
Location: Atlantic City, New Jersey
Client: Hilton Hotel Corporation
Airbrush: Paasche Model H used on sky;
    Thayer and Chandler Model A used on
    building
Ground: Strathmore cold-pressed illustration
    board
Liquid frisket: Grumbacher Miskit used to
    separate trees from background
Medium: Tube acrylics

Note: The structure was rendered in ink; the
    airbrushes were used only to apply a color
    wash. The entourage was colored using fila-
    ment brushes and tube acrylics.

Fig. 5-11. Anaheim Memorial Manor
Location: Anaheim, California
Client: Kurt Meyer F.A.I.A. & Partners
Airbrush: Paasche Model H used on sky and
   building
Ground: Crescent No. 110 illustration board
Media: Liquid and tube acrylics

Fig. 5-12. Park Place
Location: Los Angeles, California
Client: Kurt Meyer F.A.I.A. & Partners
Airbrush: Paasche Model H used on sky and
    building
Ground: Crescent No. 110 illustration board
Medium: Tube acrylics

Fig. 5-13. Phoenix Plaza
Location: Phoenix, Arizona
Client: Langdon Wilson Mumper Architects
Airbrush: Paasche Model H used on sky and
    buildings
Ground: Crescent No. 110 illustration board
Medium: Tube acrylics

Fig. 5-14. Sammis Corporate Park
Location: Parsippany, New Jersey
Client: The Sammis Company
Airbrush: Paasche Model H used on sky,
  buildings, and water
Media: Liquid and tube acrylics

Fig. 5-15. California Lutheran University
Library
Location: Thousand Oaks, California
Client: Donald DeMars Associates
Airbrush: Paasche Model H used on sky and
   building materials
Ground: Crescent No. 110 illustration board
Medium: Tube acrylics

Fig. 5-16. Anaheim Hilton
Location: Anaheim, California
Client: Hilton Hotel Corporation
Airbrush: Paasche Model VL used on sky and
    to impose transparent building washes
Ground: Crescent No. 110 illustration board
Medium: Tube acrylics

Fig. 5-17. Urban Renewal Project, Mont-
gomery Street
Location: San Francisco, California
Client: Mathew Tupaz Associates, Architects
Airbrush: Paasche Model H used on sky,
   buildings, pavement, and sidewalk
Ground: Crescent No. 110 illustration board
Liquid frisket: Grumbacher Miskit used to
   separate trees from background
Media: Dr. P.H. Martins airbrush colors used
   on background buildings; tube and liquid
   acrylics applied to brick buildings, street
   scene, and vegetation.

Fig. 5-18. Orange Center
Location: Orange, California
Client: Skidmore, Owings & Merrill
Airbrush: Paasche Model V used on buildings;
    Paasche Model H used on sky and pave-
    ment
Ground: Crescent No. 110 illustration board
Liquid frisket: Grumbacher Miskit used to
    separate foreground tree from background
Medium: Tube acrylics

Fig. 5-19. Universal Ampitheatre
Location: Universal City, California
Client: Skidmore, Owings & Merrill
Airbrush: Paasche Models V and VI
Ground: Mounted photopanel (Kodak photo-
    mural paper)
Medium: Tube acrylics

Note: Only the people were colored with fila-
    ment brushes. The rest of the illustration
    was colored with acrylics, using the rela-
    tively small V and VL model airbrushes set
    at the lowest air pressure possible. The pho-
    tomural paper used has low absorption
    much like hot-pressed illustration board.

Fig. 5-20. Manufacturing Facility
Location: Simi Valley, California
Client: Investment Building Group
Airbrush: Paasche Model H used on sky,
    clouds, and building
Ground: Crescent No. 110 illustration board
Medium: Tube acrylics

Fig. 5-21. Hayward Business Center
Location: Hayward, California
Client: Investment Building Group
Airbrush: Paasche Model H used on sky,
    building, and pavement
Ground: Crescent No. 110 illustration board
Medium: Tube acrylics

Fig. 5-22. Research and Development Park
Location: Thousand Oaks, California
Client: Investment Building Group
Airbrush: Paasche Model H used on sky,
    stucco, and glazing
Ground: Crescent No. 110 illustration board
Medium: Tube acrylics

Note: The roof tile was painted using filament
    brushes.

Fig. 5-23. Rolling Oaks Business Center
Location: Thousand Oaks, California
Client: Wilma Pacific
Airbrush: Paasche Model H used on sky,
 stucco, and glazing
Ground: Crescent No. 110 illustration board
Medium: Tube acrylics

Note: The roof materials were painted using
 filament brushes.

Fig. 5-24. Dart Square
Location: Beverly Hills, California
Client: Lomax Rock Associates Architects
Airbrush: Paasche Model H used on sky,
    building, and pavement
Ground: Crescent colored mat board
Media: Tube and liquid acrylics

Fig. 5-25. Cathedral Square
Location: Cathedral City, California
Client: McClellan Cruz Gaylord Associates,
    Architects
Airbrush: Paasche Model H used on sky,
    pavement, building base color
Ground: Crescent colored mat board
Media: Tube acrylics, colored pencils

Note: Textures applied with filament brushes
    and colored pencils

Fig. 5-26. Gemco Stores Prototype
Client: Lucky Stores Inc.
Airbrush: Paasche Model H used on sky,
   pavement, and building
Ground: Crescent No. 110 illustration board
Medium: Tube acrylics

Fig. 5-27. Safeway Stores Prototype
Client: McClellan Cruz Gaylord Associates,
 Architects
Airbrush: Paasche Model H used on sky,
 building, and pavement
Ground: Crescent colored mat board
Media: Liquid and tube acrylics

Fig. 5-28. Garden Grove Center
Location: Garden Grove, California
Client: Herbert Nadel A.I.A. Partners
Airbrush: Paasche Model H used on sky,
  building, and pavement textures
Ground: Crescent colored mat board
Medium: Tube acrylics

Fig. 5-29. 1900 Sepulveda
Location: Westwood Village, California
Client: James T. Nakoaka Associates Architects
Airbrush: Paasche Model H used on sky, building, and pavement
Ground: Crescent No. 110 illustration board
Medium: Tube acrylics

Fig. 5-30. Manhattan Beach Office Plaza
Location: Manhattan Beach, California
Client: Herbert Nadel A.I.A. Partners
Airbrush: Paasche Model H used on sky,
   building, and pavement
Ground: Crescent No. 110 illustration board
Medium: Tube acrylics

Fig. 5-31. Hilton Seapointe
Location: Shell Beach, California
Client: RRM Design Group
Airbrush: Paasche Model H used on sky,
   building, and glass reflections
Ground: Crescent No. 110 illustration board
Medium: Tube acrylics

Fig. 5-32. Hilton Seapointe Lobby
Location: Shell Beach, California
Client: RRM Design Group
Airbrush: Paasche Model H used extensively
    except on wood grain, plants, furniture, and
    people
Ground: Crescent colored mat board
Media: Tube and liquid acrylics

Fig. 5-33. Parking Structure for Office
Complex
Location: Riverside, California
Client: Langdon Wilson Mumper Associates
Airbrush: Paasche Model H used on parking
    structure
Ground: Crescent No. 110 illustration board
Media: Tube and liquid acrylics

Fig. 5-34. Office Complex
Location: Riverside, California
Client: Langdon Wilson Mumper Architects
Airbrush: Paasche Model H used on sky and
   office building
Ground: Crescent No. 110 illustration board
Media: Tube and liquid acrylics

Fig. 5-35. Moreno Valley Business Center
Location: Moreno Valley, California
Client: Benzeevi Cohen Corporation
Airbrush: Paasche Model H used on sky,
    haze, and minor textures
Ground: Crescent colored mat board
Medium: Tube acrylics

Fig. 5-36. Rancho Pacifica
Location: Los Angeles, California
Client: Herbert Nadel A.I.A. Partners
Airbrush: Paasche Model H used on sky,
    buildings, and pavement
Ground: Crescent colored mat board
Medium: Liquid and tube acrylics

Fig. 5-37. Chevron Business Complex
Location: Ontario, California
Client: Mathew Tupaz Associates, Architects
Airbrush: Paasche Model V used on sky,
    pavement, and glass highlights
Ground: Strathmore cold-pressed illustration
    board
Medium: Tube acrylics

Fig. 5-38. Warner Ridge
Location: Woodland Hills, California
Client: Herbert Nadel A.I.A. Partners
Airbrush: Paasche Model H used on sky,
   building, and pavement
Ground: Crescent No. 110 illustration board
Medium: Tube acrylics

Fig. 5-39. Ocean House
Location: Santa Monica, California
Client: Corporate Planning and Research
Airbrush: Paasche Model H used on sky and
    building
Ground: Crescent No. 110 illustration board
Medium: Tube acrylics

Fig. 5-40. Hollywood International Center
Location: Hollywood, California
Client: Mathew Tupaz Associates, Architects
Airbrush: Paasche Models V and H used on
   sky and major buildings
Ground: Crescent No. 110 illustration board
Media: Liquid and tube acrylics

Fig. 5-41. Existing Site of the Proposed
Stagecoach Plaza
Location: Thousand Oaks, California

Note: The City and County Planning Commis-
   sions require some proposed buildings to be
   presented in the form of a site photograph
   with an illustration of the new project accurately superimposed over it. Figure 5-42
   shows the finished illustration, completed
   directly on the original photograph.

Fig. 5-42. Stagecoach Plaza
Location: Thousand Oaks, California
Client: Stagecoach Properties
Airbrush: Paasche Model H used on sky,
   building, and pavement
Ground: Color reflective photograph
Media: Liquid and tube acrylics

Note: This illustration shows the intended
   widening of the street.

Fig. 5-43. Existing Site of Proposed Medical Building
Location: Thousand Oaks, California

Note: As in figure 5-41, this proposal was to
be presented in the form of a site photograph with the new project superimposed
over it. Figure 5-44 shows the completed
illustration.

Fig. 5-44. Medical Building
Location: Thousand Oaks, California
Client: Kurt Meyer, F.A.I.A. & Partners
Airbrush: Paasche Models V and H used on
    building
Ground: Color reflective photograph
Media: Liquid and tube acrylics

BIBLIOGRAPHY

Atkins, William. *Architectural Presentation Techniques*. New York: Van Nostrand Reinhold, 1976.

Burden, Ernest. *Architectural Delineation*. New York: McGraw-Hill, 1971.

Doyle, Michael E. *Color Drawing*. New York: Van Nostrand Reinhold, 1979.

Ellinger, Richard G. *Color Structure and Design*. New York: D. Van Nostrand, 1963.

Gruppé, Emile A. *Gruppé on Color*. New York: Watson-Guptill, 1979.

Guptill, Arthur. *Color in Sketching and Rendering*. New York: Reinhold Corp., 1949.

Halse, Robert O. *Architectural Rendering: The Technique of Contemporary Presentation*. New York: McGraw-Hill, 1972.

Jacoby, Helmut. *Architectural Drawing*. New York: Praeger Publishers, 1965.

————. *New Architectural Drawings*. New York: Praeger Publishers, 1969.

Kautzky, Ted. *Ways with Watercolor*. New York: Reinhold Corp., 1963.

Lin, Mike W. *Architectural Rendering Techniques*. New York: Van Nostrand Reinhold, 1985.

Misstear, Cecil, with Helen Scott-Harman. *The Advanced Airbrush Book*. New York: Van Nostrand Reinhold, 1984.

Mitooka, Eiji, and Don Design Associates. *Airbrushing in Rendering*. New York: Van Nostrand Reinhold.

Stanton, Reggie. *Drawing and Painting Buildings*. Cincinnati: North Light Publishers, 1978.

Tombs, Seng-gye C., and Christopher Hunt. *The Airbrush Book*. New York: Van Nostrand Reinhold, 1980.

Vero, Radu. *Airbrush: The Complete Studio Handbook*. New York: Watson-Guptill, 1983.

Wang, Thomas C. *Plan and Section Drawing*. New York: Van Nostrand Reinhold, 1979.

INDEX

Acrylic paint, 13, 26
Aggregate, 47–48, 112
Air
  compressors, 9, 10
  erasers, 15, 16
  flow, 25
  hoses, 10, 15, 16
  pressure indicator, 10
  pressure regulator, 10
  supply, 9–10
Airbrush
  choosing, 3–9
  holders, 15, 16
Airport hotel, 89–94
Aluminum oxide, 16
Anaheim Hilton, 131
Anaheim Memorial Manor, 126
Art Masking Fluid (Winsor & Newton), 17, 18
Art Maskoid, 17, 18
Artist Beware (McCann), 15

Badger
  Air-Opaque liquid acrylics, 12, 28, 51, 57, 58, 60, 69, 89
  GFX double-action airbrush, 5
  Silent-II air compressor, 11
  350 single-action airbrush, 3, 4
  200 single-action airbrush, 5
Benzeevi Cohen Corporation, 148
Blemishes, 106
Brick, 47–49, 107–13
  office building, 100–106
  three-dimensionality, 57
Bubbling, 31

Cadmium, 15
California Lutheran University Library, 130
Carbon dioxide, 10
Cathedral Square, 140

Chevron Business Complex, 152
Colors, 41
Compressed gas tank, 10
Compressor. *See* Air compressor
Concrete, 45
Conrad International and Jupiter's Casino, 124
Continuity, 25–26
Corporate Planning and Research, 154
Crescent No. 110 illustration board, 26
Cube, 30–35
Cylinder, 36–38

Dart Square, 139
Detail, 51–57, 60–76
Donald DeMars Associates, 130
Dots, 27
Double-action airbrushes, 3, 5
Dr. P.H. Martins, 12, 26, 132

Edges, softening and blending, 26
Equipment, 1–22
Exercises
  advanced, 43–76
  afternoon sky, 73–76
  basic, 25–41
  brick, 47–49
  brick, three-dimensionality, 57
  building detail, 51–57
  corner window, 60–68
  glass facade, 69–72
  marble, 49–51
  marble, three-dimensionality, 58–59
  precast concrete and stucco, 45–46
  solid geometric forms, 30
  warm-up, 26–29

Filament brushes, 95–99
Filipinas Plaza, 116
Finch Hall, Fuller Theological Seminary, 120
Friskets, 15
  gum arabic and, 13
  paper and, 14
  trouble-shooting tips, 18–19
  types and manufacturers, 17–18
  uses, 19–21

Garden Grove Center, 143
Gemco Stores Prototype, 141
Glass, 105, 107, 110–11. *See also* Window and concrete office building, 95–99
  facade, 69–72
  panel, 54, 56
Glendale Square Lobby, 123
Granite, 112
Graphix Prepared Frisket (Ohio Graphic Art Systems, Inc.), 17, 26
Grounds, 11, 14
Grumbacher Miskit, 17, 18
Guggenheim Museum, 37

Hayward Business Center, 136
Herbert Nadel, A.I.A. & Partners, 89–94, 100–106, 143, 145, 151, 153
Hilton Hotel and Casino, 125
Hilton Hotels Corporation, 124, 125, 131
Hilton Seapointe, 146, 147
Holbein
  Aeroflash airbrush colors, 12
  YT-02 single-action airbrush, 9
Hollywood International Center, 155

Honda Corporation headquarters, 73

Illustration board, 14
Impastos, 13
Inks, 11
Investment Building Group, 135, 136, 137
Iwata double-action airbrushes, 8, 9

James T. Nakoaka Associates Architects, 144
John Siebel, A.I.A., 95–99
Jose Francisco Soria, A.I.A., 119

Kodak photomural paper, 134
Kurt Meyer F.I.A.A. & Partners, 120, 126, 127, 159

Landscapes, 73–76, 82, 84–85
Langdon Wilson Mumper Architects, 107–13, 116, 117, 118, 121, 122, 123, 128, 149, 150
Light to dark building detail, 54–56
Lines, 27
Lomax Associates Architects, 139
Los Robles Office Building, 122
Lucky Stores Inc., 141
Luma watercolors, 12

Manhattan Beach Office Plaza, 145
Manufacturers of airbrushes, 8
Marble, 49–51, 58–59
Mathew Tupaz Associates, Architects, 132, 152, 155
McCann, Michael, 15
McLellan Cruz Gaylord Associates, Architects, 78–81, 140, 142
Media, 11–13, 26
Medical building, 82–88
Medical Planning Associates, 82–88
Miskit (M. Grumbacher), 17, 18
Mistakes, 106

Moreno Valley Business Center, 148

National Institute for Occupational Safety and Health (NIOSH), 15
Nitrogen, 10

Ocean House, 154
Orange Center, 133

Paasche
    AB turbine-driven double-action airbrush, 5, 6
    AEC air eraser, 16
    V double-action airbrush, 6
    Model H color cup, 9
    Model H #1 spray tip, 95
    Model H single-action diffuser, 3, 4, 26, 78, 82, 89, 100, 107
    Model H spray-type casting, 49
    VI double-action airbrush, 6
A Painter's Guide to the Safe Use of Materials (Seeger), 15
Park Place, 127
Pelikan drawing inks, 12
Phoenix Plaza, 128
Photographic reproduction, 13
Precast concrete, 45–46
Pressure-tank valve, 9
Propellant, 9, 10
Puddle-and-vein technique, 51
Puddling, 82

Rancho Pacifica, 151
Research and Development Park, 137
Ripple effect, 5
Rolling Oaks Business Center, 138
RRM Design Group, 146, 147
Ruling pen, 17

Safety tips, 15
Safeway Stores Prototype, 142
Sammis Company, The, 129
Sammis Corporate Park, 129
Santa Monica Medical Building, 117
Seeger, Nancy, 15

Shiva Shivair airbrush colors, 12–13
Sierra Medical Center, 118
Single-action airbrushes, 3, 5
Sketch, colored by airbrush, 78–81
Skidmore, Owings & Merrill, 133, 134
Sky-scapes, 73–76, 82–83
Spare-parts repair kit, 7
Spatter effect, 28
Sphere, 39–41
Splatter effect
    aggregate and, 47–48
    marble and, 49–50
    precast concrete and stucco, 45–46
Spray-tip assemblies, 3, 4, 95
Sputter, 7, 10
Stagecoach Plaza, 157
Stagecoach Properties, 157
Stipple, 5, 7, 95, 99, 104
Strathmore cold-pressed illustration board, 89, 107
Stucco, 45–46, 92
Surface treatments, 45–49, 51–59

Technique, 23–41
Textures, 28
Thayer & Chandler Model A double-action airbrush, 6
Three-dimensional surface treatments, 51–59
Tone, 28
    feathering, 37
    gradations of, 36

Universal Amphitheatre, 134

Warner Ridge, 153
Water, 113
Watercolors, 13
Wilma Pacific, 138
Windows, 93. See also Glass
    corner, 60–68
    facade, 89–94
Winsor & Newton Airbrush colors, 13, 69
Wright, Frank Lloyd, 37